LIVING WITH HOPE

LIVING WITH HOPE

Cardinal Carlo Maria Martini, S.J.

CATHOLIC BOOK PUBLISHING CORP.
New Jersey

NIHIL OBSTAT: Rev. Msgr. James M. Cafone, M.A., S.T.D.
Censor Librorum

IMPRIMATUR: ✠ Most Rev. John J. Myers, J.C.D., D.D.
Archbishop of Newark

This book was originally published in Italian by Giunti Editore S.p.A. under the title *Piccolo manuale della speranza. Vivere con fiducia il nostro tempo*. The English translation is by Bianca Zagolin.

The topic entitled "The Final Judgment" is taken from the book by Carlo Maria Martini entitled *The Ignatian Exercises by the Light of the Gospel of Matthew*. © AdP, Rome.

The topic entitled *"Una visuale grandiosa della fine della storia"* / *"A Grandiose View of the End of History"* is taken from the book by Carlo Maria Martini entitled "Il segreto della prima lettera di Pietro" / *"Peter's First Epistle"* 2005 © Edizioni Piemme.

"The School of the Word" translated by Matthew J. O'Connell, *Worship* (Vol. 61, 5), May 1987, and reproduced here with the permission of the publishers.

The publisher wishes to thank Marinella Ogliaruso for her valuable collaboration.

(T-167)

ISBN 978-1-937913-78-6

Printed in Canada
www.catholicbookpublishing.com

FOREWORD

Are we headed for an Apocalypse? This is the impression that many of us have as we consider the great disasters of our times and the wars and the hates that torment so many peoples. The correct response actually is "yes." Christians believe that this world must come to an end, and science confirms this belief. This is why many people fearfully ask: "Master, when will these things happen and what will be the signs that they are about to happen?" (Lk 21:7).

Jesus said that we should not be afraid: "When you hear of wars and revolutions, do not be afraid." He also said, "there will be terrifying events and great signs in the heavens" (Lk 21:9, 11) "but not even a hair on your head will be lost" (Lk 21:18). Christians can be assured that God will come to their aid. Even non-Christians can be sure of this.

Carlo Maria Martini
Corriere della Sera, March 27, 2011

CONTENTS

1

An End or a Beginning?

The End of Times

WHENEVER one era ends and another begins, whether it be the end of a period of time or a political upheaval, some people begin to think in terms that could be described as millennial or apocalyptic.

Leaving aside Biblical and literary apocalyptic texts, there have always been some people who have proclaimed that a final period of affliction was coming which would inaugurate a new age. We only have to think of the Montanists in the second century A.D., the Cathars in the Middle Ages, and the fringe groups of our own times.

In his article entitled "Apocalypse Soon" which appeared in the *Harvard Divinity Bulletin*, the historian Paul Boyer wrote that "interest in Biblical prophecy, which was never all that common in America, has greatly increased." And this is also true outside of religious circles; the laity, especially those interested in ecology, speak extensively of the coming of some great catastrophic event.

A Definition of Apocalyptic

Apocalyptic predictions tend to be anxious and fearful. But it can be difficult to pin down exactly what is meant by "apocalyptic." I would propose that one should define this word in terms of a certain uneasiness, a profound feeling that something is wrong with the way things are going. There is also the hope that things will unexpectedly improve, but not because of anything we humans have done. Rather, the improvement would come about through the intervention of some power from above. Literally, the word "apocalypse" means "reveal," "removing the veil"; it thus refers to a sudden and decisive change in the pattern of history. "Apocalyptic" also refers to the exact year and day when this event will occur. This information is communicated to humanity by a prophet who speaks in the name of some superior being, but always in cryptic language.

The apocalyptic thus involves a certain amount of fear and anxiety concerning what will happen at the end of time, but also the hope of a new beginning.

We have seen any number of apocalyptic predictions over the last couple of centuries. Some of them came from the founders of different sects, while others were the product of any number of prophecies uttered by various men or women.

Apocalyptic Language in the New Testament

One can even find apocalyptic language in the New Testament, even in places that one would not expect to find it. It would be easy to miss the fact that the number of days in the birth narrative of Jesus found in the Gospel of Luke is an allusion to the number of years after the destruction of the temple of Jerusalem until the time of a great restoration described in the Book of Daniel. This calculation in Daniel, in turn, is based upon a calculation found in Jeremiah 25 which predicted a period of expectation that would last 70 years. Daniel speaks of 70 weeks of years (62 plus 7 plus 1).

A similar sum is found in the first chapters of Luke where we hear that the annunciation to Zechariah and that to Mary were both proclaimed by the same angel Gabriel who is mentioned in the Book of Daniel as having predicted 70 weeks of years (or 490 years) from the destruction of the holy city. There are exactly 490 days from the annunciation to Zechariah to the presentation of the baby Jesus in the temple. Granted, this is a bit cryptic, but this is exactly how apocalyptic authors would communicate their message. The hidden message being communicated here is that Jesus is the dawning of the end of times. But this is proclaimed with courage and hope, not the anxiety and fear that one finds in many apocalyptic predictions past and present.

Are these days, our own times, the end of times?

We can say "yes," because Jesus has already come. But at the same time and for the same reason, there is no point in concentrating on catastrophic events. Our attitude should be marked by courage and hope. In other words, we have to distance ourselves from obscure omens and adopt a prophetic vision for our times.

The life, death, and resurrection of Jesus have given new meaning to the world, to history, and to the cosmos. Each moment offers possibilities for a new humanity. This is the only way that we can view things. We have the opportunity to work and fight for justice and love with the certainty that these will prevail. We have entered a new reality, that of the Kingdom of God which is based upon forgiveness and love. This reality will last forever; this glory will one day be revealed.

From this starting point we can live in the world with a new solidarity; we can build an economy based upon the needs of each person as opposed to being based upon competition. This is essential to insure the future of the planet.

What is needed?

Most of all, we must render glory to God for the grace of being able to live in Christian hope and to proclaim this hope to others for the good of the whole human race.

Hoping Against Every Hope

This is certainly a difficult but also an absolutely necessary task: to confront the present difficult situation in which we find ourselves with never-ending human hope. Yet, we must commit ourselves to this undertaking if we wish to avoid the discouragement and pessimism which would be a much worse alternative.

What can a Christian hope to do to better his earthly reality? What promises might one find in the Word of God in order to create a more just society? These are important questions to consider as we reflect upon the ongoing debate among the various political theologies and the theology of liberation.

In my pastoral letter *I am at the Door*, I addressed this topic in a short chapter entitled "What can we hope for upon this earth?" I would like to propose a re-consideration of what I wrote with the starting point being the double risk of reducing Christian hope either to our hope for a heavenly reward after this life or its complete anticipation here and now, as if this were the fulfillment of the Kingdom of God, a theory that some political theologies propose.

This tendency to deal with the question either in an eschatological sense or as an earthly reality is based upon an erroneous and imprecise understanding of hope. It is due to the fact that people base their hopes upon only one of its dimensions, whether it be our earthly hope or our eternal hope, ignoring the other dimension. These two dimensions of hope are intimately interconnected, even if that unity can sometimes only be perceived from the point of view of the Christian contemplative and the person of prayer.

I will therefore attempt to gradually point out why this dichotomy is erroneous. I will do this by considering four points: a comparison of hope in wealthy countries with hope experienced in underdeveloped countries; the true nature of Christian hope; the relationship between the goodness of the present era and that of the eschatological era; and the task of the Christian community.

To hope is the same as to live: a person lives inasmuch as that person hopes, and the definition of his existence is tied to the extent of his hope.

When one travels in a Third World country, one can be taken by surprise that, in spite of the sufferings caused by hunger, poverty, and illness, people are often quite happy, smiling, filled with gratitude, ready to celebrate, somehow content with their lot. It does not take much for them to break into celebration, singing and dancing although they have so, so little.

We, on the other hand, who have so much, so many gadgets that make us comfortable and spare us toil, have not yet discovered how to be grateful for what we have (even though we value these things and would like to multiply them so that everyone could have them). They seem to be little more than responses to our needs. They fall short of being signs of a bond among us, of a fraternity that is worth developing, of a desire for a more profound greater good which knocks at the doors of our minds.

One finds this openness in the cultures of poor countries: people can see the few goods that they possess symbolically and are joyfully grateful for them, seeing them as signs of a bond of solidarity which unites them with each other, of a covenant which sustains them, of a point of view, of a mutual hope.

In other words, when one considers simpler cultures, one realizes that society cannot be defined simply as a means of providing services, an accumulation of public utilities. It is not enough to provide for all of our material needs, because even when all of those things are available, it does not guarantee that people will possess the hope which they need to live and to work.

What Is Hope?

Above all, it is never hope for something, for an object. It is overall hope in someone!

When one speaks about one's hope in terms of a material object, of a response to a physical need, then hope becomes a simple wish, a yearning, a hope to get by.

Biblical hope, on the other hand, is based upon God himself who is the hope of Israel, as the Psalmist says, "You, my Lord, are my hope, my trust, my Lord from the time of my youth" (Ps 71:5). Biblical hope is a sense of certainty concerning future events which is based upon one's trust in God. Abraham, "believed, hoping against hope, and he became the father of many peoples" (Rom 4:18).

This hope recognizes the vital link between good things in the present age and those in the future, between material and spiritual blessings, between things which are visible and those which are invisible. Concretely, one can speak of the link between physical health and salvation (with all that this phrase, "salvation," means). Jesus says, "In order that you know that the Son of Man has authority upon the earth to forgive sins," thus the spiritual, invisible, and eternal dimension, "Rise, he said to the paralytic, take up your mat and go home" (Mt 9:6). The physical health which the paralytic recovers is a material, bodily, visible good, but it is not in opposition to, but rather is a sign of the salvation that was also given to this man.

There is thus an inseparable link between good things received in the present and those that will be received in the future. Present blessings promote Christian hope if they are interpreted as signs of the blessing of God and an anticipation of the goodness that will embrace man, body and spirit, in the joy of the definitive manifestation of the Kingdom. Being well off, having one's health, work, riches, the joy of living together and building a just society together are all considered by a Christian to be manifestations of the promise of God. This, however, is not a promise that we expect to have fulfilled in a particular time and place, but rather it is one that remains infallible in joy and in sorrow, in the light and in the darkness, because its ultimate goal includes also these temporary and partial fulfillments of the promise.

God is He Who promises and maintains, even when we are standing in the shadow of the cross. The price of hope is the decision to firmly believe in the promise of God and the willingness to be filled with gratitude and wonder as one perceives the gifts of this world to be an anticipation of the fulfillment of God's ultimate gift.

Life Is a Covenant

Hope is a glimpse of the fact that life is a covenant.

If one lives in Christian hope, one will perceive certain consequences concerning the good we experience in the present and that for which we hope in the future.

First of all, one can see the contrast between the present partial fulfillment of the promise here on earth and the total fulfillment that we await in the future. This provides us with the opportunity to choose hope as the fundamental option of our existence. This option is intimately tied to our option for faith. By choosing hope, one chooses to work for the good of all people, for justice, for equal opportunity, for truth, for honesty.

We can see that our present blessings, including those that are material, are a promise and a pledge of hope when we consider them to be gifts from a particular Someone. This leads us to a sense of wonder, gratitude, and appreciation. This is the only way that they can help us to establish the bonds of a just covenant. This is the only way that they can teach us about the Kingdom of God and its justice.

Appreciating the abundance of food as the victory over hunger, health as the victory over sickness, material well-being, culture, peace, the rapport between humanity and creation: appreciating all these goods is linked to the ability to see how these blessings bring us to live in covenant with other human beings. In the light of faith, this appreciation also leads us to an even more radical covenant between God and the human family, a covenant that is the only stable foundation of our covenant with other human beings.

A Culture of Hope

In *I am at the Door*, I wrote that "we must continually reevaluate the way we think and speak to recognize the bond between our earthly hopes about which the Bible often speaks and those hopes which are invisible, definitive, and which give meaning to the other hopes." Both of these hopes lead us to an attitude which is essential for our earthly lives but which is not quantifiable: wonder, friendship, the ability to recognize the goodness that surrounds us so that we might value and promote it.

All of what I have said allows for and promotes a culture of hope. Someone who looks at life this way fights for justice with love, for work for all, for a balance in our environment. That person commits him/herself to a realistic utopia, one that has been proposed by the social teaching of the Church. That person lives in the fullness of his/her life by embracing the values of the Kingdom with the certainty that they are eternal and an anticipation of that which we await with faith from God alone.

At the present moment, with all of the problems we face, we badly need hope. This is especially true of those who courageously are willing to commit themselves to the betterment of the social, economic, civil, and political dimensions of our lives.

The Christian community can and must be a type of leaven of hope. This should be true not only in its proclamation of the eternal truths, nor only in its promotion of solidarity (which is urgently needed). The community can contribute to maintaining and fostering hope by addressing some things which are often forgotten and ignored: the bond of covenant, trust of others, wonder, and a reciprocal welcoming spirit which, from the earliest moments of one's family life, establish the bonds that unite one person to another. These are attitudes that must be acknowledged and promoted lest they languish and even disappear, extinguishing joy and hope even in the midst of a relative abundance of material goods which nevertheless cannot fill the void in the hearts of men.

I think that if Abraham knew how to hope beyond hope, it might be possible for us to overcome difficult moments and to arrive at calmer shores. I pray that no one fail in this task.

The Persistence of the Patience of God

The mystery of the bond between the heavens and the earth can be understood in light of the Ascension of Jesus into the heavens. He who descended among us and became the Son of Man ascended into the heavens so that every person might be elevated to the dignity of Son of God.

In Jesus, our older brother, we too enter into the joy of the Father. Having died and been buried with Him in our Baptism, we rise with Him and are seated at the right hand of the Father. Our life is hidden with Christ in God.

This is why we look for the things which are above (Col 3:2f): where our treasure lies is where our heart is to be found (Mt 16:21). This is where we want to live forever.

The mystery of the Ascension reveals the final goal of creation and the redemption. God made man and became human so that man might become Godlike. Christ is the first fruits. All flesh is invited to embrace its original beauty in Him, and all history arrives at its glorious destiny in Him.

This is a mystery that has much to teach us, especially when we are living in an era in which we do not seem to know from where we have come and where we are headed. Without past and without a future, people today feel uneasy and distressed, as if they were floating in mid-air. People seem to have the impression that they have come from nothing and are heading to nothing. They suffer from a "religious alienation," but in a different way than that which people experienced a century ago. They are not estranged from religion, but rather of religion. If at one time religion estranged one from things, today those things estrange one from religion. God seems to be a limb that was amputated that causes phantom pain, but a pain that is as vast as one's very existence. It is as infinite as God Himself, his being, which has been amputated from our lives.

Modern man seems to be in the grip of nothingness. He is devoured from within by his own void, and from without by an infinite variety of things. While he can control everything, he nevertheless feels himself to be estranged from everything, far away from his chosen homeland.

Christ, ascending to the heavens, distributes his gifts upon the earth (Eph 4:8). His first gift is to present Himself as the source of true meaning for our lives and our history.

The return of the Son to the heavens opens up the way to reach Him and marks the birth of brothers upon the earth. The Spirit Whom He will send will make them sons of the Father, brought to full maturity so that they might be witnesses and continue his mission to the very ends of the earth.

We accompany the disciples who went out from Jerusalem to take a Sabbath's day trip.

The Kingdom of God

Jesus revealed Himself to be the Living One for forty days. He taught about the Kingdom, explaining the Scriptures which speak about the mystery of his death and Resurrection. We last see Him upon the Mount of Olives. The trees there had seen his humble and yet glorious entrance into Jerusalem, his vigil throughout the night and his mortal agony as He prepared for his crucifixion. Here one sees both the fullness of joy and expectation.

"Lord, is this the time to establish the Kingdom of Israel?" This is the last question that the disciples asked Him. This was something that had been burning within their hearts. Even the Pharisees asked Him, "When will the Kingdom of God arrive?" As they approached the Holy City, they thought that it would appear at any time.

Jesus answered the first question by saying that the Kingdom was already present, but in a way that they had not expected (Lk 17:20ff). He answered the second question by speaking of a long trip to a distant land (Lk 19:11ff).

The Church was born as a response to this essential question. How she understands herself and how she deals both with God and the world is based upon her response to this question. This is why it is so important to keep in mind how Jesus wants her to respond. Otherwise, even if it is with good intentions, she will show herself to be shallow and will end up doing things that retard the coming of the Kingdom. "Lord, is this the time to establish the Kingdom?" This is our own question, the question posed by the Church in every era.

The Kingdom is both the great desire of the disciples and the core of the preaching of Jesus. But what a difference there is in how they understand the term! Everyone was expecting a Messiah Who would be the king. In the name and power of God He would defeat their enemies and reign. He would establish a new era of justice, freedom, and universal peace. What could be nicer? Is this not exactly what all people hope for and what God has promised us?

Everyone, including the Baptist, thought that the Messiah would enforce the judgment of God: the victory of good over evil, the reward of the good and the punishment of those who are evil. Those who were foolish would be shamed on account of their foolishness while the wise would be honored. Once and for all the tangle of history would be resolved with the triumph over ignorance and evil, with the victory of good and wisdom. Is this not the secret desire, and sometimes not even all that secret, that the Church has had and that she has had to recognize as mistaken from her earliest days?

Purifying Our Concept of the Kingdom

We need a long purification. Even Jesus had to resolve this question for Himself. This is why He went off into the desert and why He died on the Cross. He is the Son Who brought the mercy of God down here upon the earth. His Kingdom consists in loving his brothers and sisters and healing their hurts. The only way that He knew of doing this was by giving witness to the tender love of the Father toward all even to the point of his own death. It is the path of martyrdom, that of giving witness, which He proposed to his disciples.

As Messiah He sought to heal even those who were evil of that which afflicted them, but his only weapon in this battle was the Cross upon which He bore the sin of the world. It was the role of a "weak Messiah" based upon the love of God that is given to all God's children without limit. He respectfully gives each person the liberty to embrace it.

Every misery, no matter how great it might be, is nothing else than the measure of his mercy.

The manner through which Jesus chose to give birth to his Kingdom proved problematic. It was difficult for people to accept, whether they be leaders or followers, disciples or their successors, Israel or the Church, believers or non-believers. This is why He was and still is rejected both by his enemies and his friends.

The Kingdom of God is a seed. As such, it is small. It is taken and thrown into the garden. It is yeast. It is hidden in the dough of this world (Lk 13:21). It resembles Jesus, as must the disciples and the Church who wish to give witness to Him. The world considered Him to be small and insignificant. The religious world considered Him to be unclean and despised. He "was crucified on account of our weakness" (2 Cor 13:4). Taken, thrown, and hidden in the tomb, a leaven for the earth. There He split open to give birth to the tree of life that now reaches out to the heavens.

Jesus used solidarity and compassion to bring about his Kingdom. He shared the pain of our wounds. This reveals who He and God are: mercy.

Is this the time for the dawning of the Kingdom? This question also means: what is the sense of our history that seems to continuously roll along in the same old way? What salvation is being offered to this world which is so wounded?

Jesus gives a response. First of all, He says, "Do not expect to know the time or the season that the Father has established by his own authority" (Acts 1:7). This means that the time and possibility of the dawning of the Kingdom rests in the hands of someone we can trust, for He is our Father and the Lord of creation. The Kingdom of God is God's and not ours. This alone should free us from our anxiety and fear.

God existed before this world and before history. He alone knows it to its core and guides it for the good of all his children. He loves it infinitely. We have to give up the idea of knowing a time or a chosen season in which the Kingdom will dawn or the world will come to an end. The only chosen time is that which is: the present moment in which we are called to live as children and as brothers and sisters. Anyone who dreams of some other time is trying to make the Christian faith into a fantasy.

God is presence. He is not found in the nostalgic remembrances of the past or in a flight toward the future. Christ ascended to the heavens and He was made Lord of the past and future of the promise of God. Each of us is called to live the fullness of the promise in the present.

This is why Jesus says: "You will receive power when the Holy Spirit descends upon you" (Acts 1:8). "Spirit" means breath, life. "Holy" means separate, that is, God. Receive the breath, the life of God.

The ineffable love of the Father and the Son descend upon us. It gives us life and makes us like Jesus: children capable of loving the Father and our brothers and sisters. This Spirit of Jesus marks the end of the old world and begins a new one. It is the Kingdom already present among us.

Witness and Martyrdom

"You will be my witnesses." The Greek word "martyr" means someone who remembers and gives witness. The disciples remember their master and they always have Him in their thoughts and hearts. They remembered Him and gave witness to Him in their daily lives up to the end of their lives. The Kingdom is this "witness, martyrdom." It is not some strategy or plan, whether it be earthly or religious. It is simply the fruit of the Spirit of Jesus which permits us to do and teach what He Himself did and taught.

"To the ends of the earth": these are Jesus' last words. The Kingdom is not restricted to a privileged group. The Father loves all his children without exception. The person who possesses the Spirit of Jesus already knows the love of the Father. That person therefore loves everyone, whether it be someone who is privileged or needy, a sinner, a stranger or even an enemy. The person living in God's love knows that the Father wants his home to be full (Lk 14:23) so that no one will miss out on the meal. That person knows that the house is not full until everyone is there. This is why the Church is not a collection of those who are "good" but who act as if they are either defending their castles or trying to conquer someone else's. We have to be open to everyone. "Catholic" means universal, and "apostolic" means invited, for all are invited. If we close our hearts to even one of our brothers or sisters, we are shutting out the Lord Who made Himself the last and least of all.

"When he had said this, as they were looking on, he was lifted up, and a cloud took them from their sight" (Acts 1:9). After He had invited all of his brothers and sisters, Jesus had nothing left to say. The revelation was over. God had already said everything. He only had to send down his Spirit so that they could understand what He had said and live it.

Jesus, once his mission was over, disappeared and moved off stage. When He was among us, He showed us the way. When He returned to the Father,

He showed us the goal and gave us the ability to arrive there. The cloud that hid Him reveals a new way to be present. It reminds us of the presence of God in the Exodus. He does not leave us alone. He guides us along the way until we reach our destination. From now on, every step forward is headed toward the Promised Land.

The Reaction of the Disciples

The disciples "were looking intently at the sky as he was going" (Acts 1:10). Their hearts were already reaching up to the heavens. Heaven is our homeland. It is from there that we await our Savior, the Lord Jesus Christ, who will transform our poor bodies to conform them to his glorious body, for all has been placed under his authority (Phil 3:20ff).

But this attitude has its ambiguities and dangers. The disciples first of all made the mistake of awaiting an earthly kingdom. Now they were running the opposite risk: to expect a heavenly kingdom to descend from on high. The challenge of a Christian faith is to live in this world with the Spirit which Jesus has given to us. It is possible to fervently await a heavenly reign while we are living with an all too earthly spirit.

The angels asked the disciples, "Why are you standing there looking at the sky?" (Acts 1:10). An adult faith assumes a sense of responsibility for this world, but without a worldly spirit. Now is the time for the Kingdom. There has already been a long journey throughout history on its way to the Lord. We must use the gifts and talents that He has given us in the here and now. We are called to give witness to Him so that the whole world might adore and love Him. Now is the time of his return and at the same time of our journey towards Him.

"Maran atha" come, Lord!" (1 Cor 16:22). This is the prayer and the desire of every disciple. It is the message of the bride to the groom, of all of humanity to the Lord. He is already approaching upon the same path that He trod before. The Lord is returning in the same way that He went away. We know his path. We only have to walk it.

If the Lord Who was assumed into heaven has not yet returned, it is not because "he delays his promise, as some regard delay, but he is patient with you, not wishing that any should perish, but that all should come to repentance" (2 Pet 3:9).

Time goes on, and history does not stop. But now time is part of salvation history. God, having gathered in the first of his sons, has been persistent in his patience as He awaits the return of all of his children.

It is then that the mystery of the Ascension will be fully realized. Christ Jesus, our Lord, will be our head, and we will all be his members and God will be all in all (1 Cor 15:28).

The Apocalypse of Evil

The topic of evil has always been part of our human existence from the days when Cain raised a violent hand against Abel and killed him (Gen 4:8) and God declared, "But whoever kills Cain will suffer seven times as much," (Gen 4:15) up until the words of Jesus: "Peace I leave you, my peace I give you" (Jn 14:27).

This topic has returned to center stage lately. We know the facts: horrible terrorist attacks reveal an unheard level of hate and fanaticism which can now draw upon the latest technology and which nourish themselves with novel forms of civil and religious fundamentalism (we only have to think of all those who aspire to be suicide bombers). Following the terrorist attacks, there tends to be a witch hunt for terrorists that ends up in more violence.

These things sadden us, leave us confused and shaken. We mourn the numberless dead, those whose wounds will leave scars that will never be healed, the families torn apart, the millions of refugees, and the tears of mutilated children.

We have so many questions, hypothesis, worries. We are bothered at a human, religious, and political level. We want to understand, judge, know what to do to end the terrorism, the fear, the wars. What can we do to find a lasting peace?

The situation is of course too complex and fluid to describe adequately. Each day we hear the news, much of it sad. This is why I seriously asked myself and I asked the Lord if in this present whirlwind we can truly speak about peace? How, and what will it cost?

Speaking, reading, and listening extensively, I have come to see how different people's opinions are. There are so many ideas, so many ways of seeing things. One hears passionate, highly emotional responses. People don't want to surrender their prejudices, especially those of which they are not even aware. It would seem wiser to wait, pray, and heal the wounds as much as one can. But St. Ambrose did not hide away to reflect upon and judge the public and controversial events of his own days. So I, his humble successor, ask, through his intercession and with the prayers and suggestions of many, the grace to be able to raise my voice concerning these things before God, before the Gospels, and before humankind.

Jesus' Reaction

I would like to use as my starting point a passage in the Gospel of Luke which contains two affirmations or reactions on the part of Jesus when He was confronted by bloody deeds due to actions by the state and by natural calamities.

> At that time, some people were speaking about what had happened to some Galileans whose blood Pilate had poured out upon their sacrifices. Arising to speak, Jesus said to them "Do you believe that these Galileans were the worst sinners in all of Galilee because of what happened to them? No, I tell you, but if you do not repent, you will perish in the same way. Or those eighteen people who were killed when the tower in Shiloh collapsed. Do you think that they were guiltier than all of the other inhabitants in Jerusalem? No, I tell you, but if you do not repent, you will all perish in the same way.
>
> —Lk 13:1-5

We should note a curious fact. St. Ambrose, who up to this point has been meticulous in his commentary upon the third Gospel, seems to be a bit evasive concerning these verses. Asking himself whether Pilate might have killed these men because of some anti-Roman action on their part, St. Ambrose limits himself to a marginal note in which he hypothesizes that the massacre in Jerusalem was due to some ritual uncleanness of the Galileans. He thought that this was an example of a punishment "upon those who at the inspiration of the devil offer sacrifices with an unclean spirit" (*Exposition of the Gospel of Luke*, VII). He avoids commenting on the messy politics and theological questions that arise in this scene and he doesn't even speak about Jesus' unusual and troubling response. We, on the other hand, cannot afford to follow his example.

Jesus was being confronted with tangled ethical, theological, and political questions. This reminds one of the question that He was asked concerning paying taxes to Caesar (Lk 20:20-26), although this situation is certainly weightier. When Luke speaks of the latter instance, he specifically mentions that those questioning Him were seeking to trap Him, pretending to seek the just response. They wanted to catch Him making an imprudent response which they could then report to the civil officials to have Him arrested (Lk 20:20).

Here, in a similar way, there is the question which is also a trap, but it involves a much more troubling situation. Here we are talking about a massacre executed by a representative of the emperor within the sacred quarters of the temple. It probably happened during the Passover celebration during which a number of people were massacred, some of whom were perhaps terrorists ready to make the ultimate sacrifice. We don't know exactly how many were killed at this time, but some years before a predecessor of Pilate had killed three thousand Jews.

Jesus is thus challenged to give his opinion. Would He condemn political assassination which was intended to humiliate the Jews and desecrate their temple? Would He condemn the cruelty and the cynicism of the governing authorities? Or would He express the opinion of many others in Israel who considered their domination by a foreign power to be better than the possible chaos that might erupt if they were to gain their freedom? Might He therefore speak of the massacre as being a regretful but necessary legitimate act, an inevitable act of repression that prevented further terrorist acts?

Even the prophet Jeremiah had once discouraged useless acts of resistance aimed at the Babylonian conquerors. I would think that Jesus must have realized that He was being asked the same question that the Jews would later explicitly address to Him: "How long will You keep us in suspense? If You are the Christ, tell us." In this case, they are saying to Him: You know everything. Tell us what the truth is, where justice lies. Then there is the second occurrence narrated in Luke (13:1-5) that reminds us of things that still happen today. It concerns a natural disaster, the collapse of a tower in Jerusalem in which eighteen people died. Then, as now, these sorts of things raise a number of questions. Was this disaster unavoidable, or was it the product of some act of negligence or a human error? Was this due to irresponsibility, or to inexcusable carelessness? Who is guilty? Who should have been vigilant? Which person in charge failed in his responsibilities, or didn't heed warnings?

These two situations were brought to Jesus' attention so that He might take a position. Some were hoping that He would condemn the tyrant Pilate. Others wanted Him to criticize the Galileans as worthless terrorists. With the collapse of the tower, He might have fervently denounced the carelessness of the governing authorities, or maybe He would condemn the imprudence of the people involved. But Jesus responds in an unexpected way. He doesn't take a position either in favor of or against any of those involved. He doesn't say who should be considered to be responsible. But He does proclaim a judgment which we must now examine. He avoids speaking about all of the serious current political issues. That probably surprised some, disturbed and angered others. What does this have to offer us for our own day? His reaction reaffirms something we can find in a recent history of the origins of Christianity: "Compared to the classical prophets, the historic Jesus is notably silent concerning many of the inflammatory issues of his days. . . . The historic Jesus not only undermines some ideologies, He undermines all ideologies" (J.P. Meier, *A Marginal Hebrew*).

Our Response Today

Something similar is happening today. The questions concerning history and even more the current dramas of our times are understandably packed with the weight of emotional suffering, with automatic responses based on our feelings, and even with prejudices. We often examine the words of some moral authority for immediate answers to clarify the situation (although this is often done to confirm what one has already decided). We have so many questions about what we are constantly seeing and hearing on the TV.

A first question concerns the perpetrators of acts of terrorism, beginning with those that are the most horrendous and homicidal, especially those that involved the suicide of the terrorist. We ask why. How could a human being be so cruel and so blind? Where in the maze of their consciences could such feelings of hate, political and religious fanaticism take root? What personal resentments and collective feelings of humiliation could be the source of such wrong-headed decisions? Nothing and no one could ever justify their actions or give them even the tiniest degree of legitimacy. But nevertheless we have to ask: have we ever taken into consideration how explosive personal and national resentments could become over time? Have we considered how our own actions can and have contributed to kindling outbursts of rebellion and hate?

I cannot ignore those who bear a great burden of responsibility for they have been blessed with material wealth and have learned how to exploit these resentments by supplying weapons, by financing terrorists, and by organizing their activities in every part of the world, and possibly even in our own neighborhoods. They have no right to do this; they have so little legitimization for their actions. We could apply to them the saying of Jesus concerning those who exploit the weaknesses of those who are simple: "they should tie a millstone around their necks and throw themselves into the depth of the sea" (Mt 18:6).

We could also consider what Jesus said during the Sermon on the Mount when He said that even an insult contains the kernel of hate and murder (Mt 5:22: "Whoever calls his brother a fool will be thrown into the fires of Gehenna"). Those of us who have reached a certain age can remember the early days of rebellion (the late 60s and early 70s) when even those who were responsible for judging and punishing would overlook and treat lightly minor acts of vandalism and disrespect toward public property and how this opened the path to more serious and even murderous actions. He who today is not punished for throwing a stone will tomorrow feel that it is acceptable to set a bomb or shoot a pistol. There has to be a "zero tolerance" for words and actions of hate; this is a Gospel injunction.

Thus, we need a severe moral and human judgment concerning every small sign of disrespect and hate, wherever it comes from and against whomever it is demonstrated. This might unmask and exorcise and disarm what lies behind it. In addition, there is a second more political and military question: will the means used to combat terrorism be effective? Will they really discourage the terrorists, make them give up on their macabre use of human bombs? Will they create the conditions in which we can overcome the causes of all of this tension?

Very few of us have certain and well-thought-out answers to these questions. They are both complex and the background and activities they address are various and changeable. They certainly weigh heavily upon everyone's consciences, and especially those of the people who are more directly responsible for the development of anti-terrorism programs with all of the political, economic, juridical, and cultural dimensions with which they must deal. They are the ones who really know when and how effective, how positive and negative, are the bombings and other forms of warfare used against terrorism, for the media only has a very limited access to the details and military strategies involved. We wouldn't dare give an answer to all of this here, but it is closely connected to what follows.

The third question is an ethical one. Are the techniques used in the fight against terrorism, especially when it involves violence, proportionate acts of legitimate defense, or in some cases do they seem to be excessive and primarily acts of revenge? Clearly, we cannot deny the right of a legitimate defense to anyone, not even when we are speaking of a Gospel-based principle. But we have to keep constantly on watch to control our individual and collective passions to make sure that the necessary preventive actions we take are not based upon revenge and are not disproportionate. Have the desire for victory and the dynamism of violence at times overcome the need to be vigilant so that violent actions are executed for reasons other than our original objectives and are aimed at unarmed populations?

This is when we have to question ourselves concerning the principle of a legitimate defense, because we cannot ignore its limitations with impunity and not create more hate and conflicts than that with which we started. This sadly seems to be the case in what continues to happen all too often in the Middle East. On the one hand, there is a mad and suicidal attack on peaceful citizens, among whom many are children. This terrorism produces nothing more than more anger, indignation, and horror.

On the other hand, there are the reprisals that are difficult to classify as acts of legitimate defense when they are taken against unarmed populations, many of whom are children. Then, on top of all that, there are actual acts of war. Even the most impartial observer, sincerely convinced of the need for complete security for the country that wages these wars, is unable to see how peace and security are served by such initiatives. And yet, peace and security are also the desire of all the people whose survival is essential for future peace in the region and throughout the world.

These three questions are important to many people, and we could speak about them at quite some length. Each of them, although they have a most important ethical dimension, is nevertheless not the concern only of the Church. The Church cannot make the final pronouncement upon actions concerning which only a few people know their full purpose and extent.

By voicing these questions, I did not intend to make any definitive judgment as much as to help myself and you to reflect seriously upon them. Furthermore, I would like to encourage the competent authorities to weigh all their options and actions upon the rigorous balance of justice and the respect of the human rights of each and every person. The number of those in charge is not all that great. There are probably fewer of them than one would think or what one would deduce from the numerous theories advanced concerning them. There are really only a few people who know all the details concerning the terrorists, their plans, their resources. There is not all that much accurate information concerning the war being waged against them and how it is going, the nature of the resistance it is encountering, and the dimensions of its strategies. The political and military authorities who are responsible for these things face an arduous, lonely task as they make decisions that will literally affect millions of people.

This is why it is of tremendous importance for these actions to be decided in a stable and methodical democratic manner by legislators and by well-informed public opinion that are cognizant of the scope and extent of the eventual interventions.

What Would Jesus Say?

Here we should once again consider the attitude of Jesus in the passage from Luke that we have been discussing and to which we now return. There is another question to ask that goes beyond those concerning terrorism and war. This question is actually quite simple and Gospel based. It is: what would Jesus say today to what we have said so far? What would He suggest to us in the spirit of the Sermon on the Mount, in terms of the Beatitudes that speak of the merciful and those who work for peace?

In Luke (13:1-5), Jesus refuses to address the questions that those who spoke with Him had concerning who was the guilty party for the bloodshed. He knew that their question was actually an attempt to name a scapegoat. Instead of giving a categorical moral judgment upon individuals or groups, Jesus addresses the profound source of all of these bad things: the sinfulness of all people, the willingness of each and every person to participate internally in violence and evil. He twice repeats the phrase: "If you do not repent, you will all perish in the same way." He invites all of us to examine ourselves concerning our complicity in injustice. He admonishes us not to root it out here and there, but to change our values and our lives.

At first glance, that can surprise us. It seems like He is avoiding speaking about the present situation. He is speaking in a manner that seems to bypass the urgent need to make decisions and judgments. He seems to be generalizing in a way that could confuse wrong and right, murderer and victim, grouping them all under a common denominator.

But Jesus has no intention of releasing anyone from his own concrete responsibility. Each person is responsible for his own actions and has to bear the consequences. This is why Jesus told Peter who was trying to defend Him by force when He was being arrested: “Put your sword back where it belongs, because those who take up the sword will die by the sword” (Mt 26:52). He knows that each of us must make his own moral decision in every situation. He wants to make it clear that human attempts to combat evil with force will never have a lasting effect if we do not seriously admit that the profound causes of evil are found inside of ourselves, in the heart and life of each person, ethnic group, nation, and institution that allows injustice. If we don’t address these dwelling places of evil, changing our values, we will quickly find ourselves again facing the very evils that we tried to eliminate with our external efforts.

Overcoming the Spirit of Conflict

There are so many practices of evil to deplore and defeat. There is terrorism and violence. There are all those injustices which should be condemned. Every affront to human dignity should be eliminated. We ask ourselves: Is it really possible to turn these things around? We have to dare to say yes, for this overturning of values is necessary to overcome the spirit of conflict which will lead to the reciprocal destruction of those involved. But also, we must depend upon the grace of God and the fairness in the hearts of men.

Furthermore, we are Christians (even if we in the Western world who were once firm in this belief and lately have become more uncertain and lacking in supernatural hope); we believe that if evil abounds, then the grace of conversion and pardon will super-abound. While we leave the timing of this to the Lord of history, we nevertheless know that the conditions necessary for a life change and the adoption of a new set of values can take place in the West, possibly even as a response to these dramatic events.

One newspaper spoke of this type of awakening as an apocalypse, using the etymological sense of the word which means to "raise the veil" or "a revelation" (Enzo Bianchi, "The Apocalypse of September 11th" *La Repubblica*, October 27, 2001). It spoke of a revelation of the evil in which we are submerged, of the absurdity of the society based upon the almighty dollar, of living a life punctuated by the openings of the various world stock exchanges. This is a society which has become ridiculous in its desire for virtual investments, of transactions that are nothing more than brokered speculations. Furthermore, this society has the effrontery to export this idea all throughout the world as if it were a new form of messianism.

This type of globalization has to be rejected. A short time ago Fr. Tommasso Padoa Schioppa wrote, "the road which leads to security is longer than that which leads to Kabul. The road is also more arduous, because we are the ones who have to travel upon it, not the military or some distant land. Taking this road means being willing to change the way we live, the way we think, the way we organize our political systems. We have to ask ourselves, have we set out upon it yet?" (*Corriere della Sera*, November 18, 2001).

If this is true for the economic and political world, why should the world of morality not open itself to new horizons with a commitment to serenity and justice, to a more profound reflection on the meaning of life, to a greater openness to the mystery of God? Has God not "shut up all in disobedience" in these never-ending conflicts so that we might be "merciful toward all?" (Rom 11:32).

It is not really all that important to know if it will happen soon. As Dietrich Bonhoeffer said, "for those who are responsible the ultimate question is not, 'how can I heroically win in this situation' but rather 'what can life be like for the next generation?' It is only by asking this historically responsible question can one hope to produce fruitful solutions" (*Resistance or Surrender*, Milan, San Paolo Edizioni, 1996).

If we refuse to commit ourselves to a radical shift of values so that peace, solidarity, a willingness to live and let live, a mutual acceptance, reconciliation of differences, fraternal dialog among politicians and diplomats, while at the same time we commit violent reprisals, then we will have to face new forms of violence and terrorism. We might extinguish them for a time, but they will mercilessly rise up in other places and times. We have to disarm not only our hands but also our consciences and our hearts.

Pope John Paul II on December 4, 2001, speaking of the Middle East, said, "Violence is never resolved in conflicts. This only intensifies the problem with dramatic consequences."

Violence and evil exist everywhere, and they are at the root of it all. But good bounds forth from a more profound spring. It continually waters, heals, and gives new birth to the roots of evil and bitterness. This is why it is important to remember that each of us has to do his or her part. We each have to listen to the appeal which reaches our ears. The dramatic circumstances in which we find ourselves are a strong call to conversion and an acknowledgment of the fact that we co-exist with evil in this world. Let me underline that this is everyone's evil, not just that of people living at a certain latitude or only of those who live in the Western world. Certainly, it is there that we find its worst mistakes, its blindness, its idols, its illusions of omnipotence. This is why the Church, even that based in the Western world, has historically and still today has tried to infuse its spirit in the world. But it has never completely identified itself with any area or culture, even those with a glorious tradition of liberty and human dignity which nevertheless also are plagued by an irrational individualism, the cult of money, of success, of the image one projects, and of power.

In spite of all this, we have to remember that we in the Western world are not the only ones whom Jesus has called to change our ways. The Lord twice says in Luke, "If you do not change your ways, you will all perish." The madness of self-destruction that is found in so many dimensions of our modern culture is a danger to us all. The specters of corruption, misgovernment, private or tribal interests superseding those of the public, of dictatorship and of the primacy of the force of arms suck the life out of countless poor people in the world.

It would be all too easy to find one scapegoat and one victim. Weeds and wheat are profoundly mixed in every corner of the planet. Jesus knows the evil that is hidden in the heart of each man and each culture. He knows that this is an "unbelieving and perverse generation" (Mt 17:17). We have to acknowledge that the plagues which afflict the world (among which one could speak of war and terrorism which are a manifestation of the problem) are not only the fault of one person or another, one group of people be they near or far or another. We are all, each in our own way, co-responsible for the situation in which we find ourselves.

If in the midst of these tragic events which we wouldn't even have wanted to imagine we hear the invitation of Jesus to change our set of values and the way we judge things, we will have given birth to a society that is more thoughtful. Our young will be less debauched, less desperate to be entertained. They will be conscious of the responsibility for the future of the planet. They will be more ready to listen to the call to open their hearts so that they might be consecrated totally to the service of God and neighbor. We can already be joyful witnesses to this positive change if we look around and judge what we see with a hope-filled vision.

I cannot finish this presentation without returning for a moment to the principal inspiration that we have examined from its start: the great goodness of peace. We began by listening to what Jesus (and the Church) had to say about violence because there is one thing that is at the heart of it all: peace!

The Great Goodness of Peace

Peace is the greatest human good because it is the sum total of all the messianic goods. As peace is the synthesis of all good things, war is the synthesis and the symbol of all evil. We can never desire war for itself for it is the systematic violation of substantial human rights. There are always some cases of a legitimate defense of irrefutable goods. But these instances must be measured by the willingness to apply strict limits to what is necessary to defend oneself. At times courageous acts and interventions of inherent humanitarianism might be necessary to restore and maintain peace in situations where it is gravely at risk. But this is not yet peace.

Peace is not simply the absence of conflict, the cessation of hostilities, an armistice. It is not even the rejection of offensive words and actions (Mt 5:21-24), not even acts of forgiveness and refusal to pursue revenge or a refusal to argue (Mt 5:38-47). Peace is the product of a long lasting and sincere covenant (an enduring covenant and not only an enduring freedom). It is based upon the covenant that God made in Christ by which He forgave our sins. He healed us and gave us the possibility to become his partners in friendship and dialog so that all who love Him might be one.

In this unity and this covenant, each person sees how much we are all alike, how we are loved and forgiven. If a Christian gazes at the face of the other, he will see a reflection of the glory of Christ and the splendor of the Trinity. He can say to his brother or sister: you are incredibly important to me; what I have is yours. I love you more than I love myself. What you have is more important to me than what I have. Because your good is so important to me, everyone's good is important to me. The good of a new humanity is important to me, and not just the good of my family, or clan, or tribe, or race, or ethnic group, or movement, or party or nation. This is peace.

Every action committed against this common good is rooted in fear, jealousy, and distrust. It gives rise to conflict and nourishes hates which cause wars. We are going to need an entire history and even a super-history to accomplish this task. But this is the peace that is the goal of our human journey.

We desperately need to find within ourselves a fountain overflowing with peace that helps us to trust in the possibility of concrete and simple steps toward a change in the values and ways of judging reality. This is the only serious way to journey toward peace. We have to avoid the danger of permitting ourselves to be muddled in a climate of consumerism which keeps us from asking the important questions that have arisen because of these dramatic events. We have to commit ourselves to the art of dialog if we hope not to be dragged into cultural incomprehension. This depends on a profound self-knowledge and the ability to express this to others without resorting to prejudices, quibbles, and incomprehension.

We have to know about other religions, especially Judaism and Islam. We have to examine their history, their literature, their spiritual wealth, their mystical depths, the many ways, including social and political, in which they are lived.

Above all, we have to learn words, gestures, and acts of forgiveness, understanding, and peace. We have to use zero tolerance on any action that expresses xenophobia, anti-Semitism, and disrespect for other religious feelings and traditions. This means that others must also respect and esteem those religious signs that were and still are the ways and means by which we offer hospitality and peace to all.

May all the young people of the world be sentinels of the morning that announces the much desired day of peace.

2

Standing on the Threshold

God's Plan Will Be Achieved

ESCHATOLOGICAL views, which are common towards the end and the beginning of the liturgical year in both the Ambrosian and the Roman rituals, create different problems. In this type of view, we notice most of all our cultural distance from some passages of the Bible, even though we understand their importance.

Chapter 21 in *Luke* is written under the influence, not only of Jesus' words, but also of the catastrophic events that happen to the Jewish people, starting with the fall of Jerusalem that seems to be an omen of the end of time. After two thousand years, it is obviously difficult to recreate the troubled atmosphere in which people lived then. Although we ourselves live in troubled times, every moment in history is different. It is therefore important that we put in the right context the warnings that Jesus gave to be vigilant, for the coming of the Kingdom was at hand. These warnings, still valid today, are about the theological, not temporal, imminence of the Kingdom; that means, for each one of us, the individual imminence in the mystery of our own death and, for the world, the imminence of God's judgment that awaits humanity.

In spite of the difficulties to which I alluded above, let us try and delve into the structure of the text and possibly into its meaning for today.

5 And as some spoke of the temple, how it
was adorned with costly stones and gifts, he
said: 6 As for these things which you behold,
the days will come in which there shall not be
left one stone upon another, that shall not be
thrown down. 7 And they asked him, saying,
Master, but when shall these things be? And
what sign will there be when these things
shall come to pass? 8 And he said: Take heed
that you be not deceived, for many shall
come in my name, saying, I am Christ; and
the time draws near; therefore, do not go
after them.

9 But when you shall hear of wars and
revolutions, be not terrified: for these things
must first come to pass; but the end is not by
and by.

10 Then he said to them: nation shall rise
against nation, and kingdom against king-
dom. 11 And great earthquakes shall be in dif-
ferent places, and famines, and pestilences;
and fearful sights and great signs shall there
be from heaven.

12 But before all these, they shall lay their
hands on you, and persecute you, delivering
you up to the synagogues, and into prisons,
bringing you before kings and rulers for my
name's sake. 13 And you will be asked for a
testimony. 14 Settle it therefore in your hearts
not to meditate before what you shall answer.

> [15] For I will give you words and wisdom,
> which all your adversaries shall not be able
> to refute nor resist. [16] And you shall be be-
> trayed by parents and brethren, by relatives
> and friends; and some of you shall they put to
> death. [17] And you shall be hated by all men
> for my name's sake. [18] But not one hair on
> your head shall perish. [19] Your patience will
> save your soul.
>
> [20] And when you shall see Jerusalem sur-
> rounded by armies, then know that its desola-
> tion is near. [21] Then let those who are in Judea
> flee to the mountains; and let those who are in
> the city depart from it; and let not those who
> are in the country return to the city. [22] For these
> are the days of vengeance, that all things
> which are written may be fulfilled.
>
> [23] But woe unto women who are with
> child or those who are nursing in those days!
> For there shall be great distress in the land
> and wrath upon this people. [24] And they shall
> fall by the edge of the sword, and shall be led
> away captive into all nations, and Jerusalem
> shall be trodden down by Gentiles, until the
> times of the Gentiles be fulfilled.
>
> —Lk 21:5-24

First of all, it must be remembered that Luke distinguishes between Jesus' different eschatological sayings, unlike Mark and Matthew who have linked different sayings into a single one. In Chapter 17, verses 22-37, he deals with the day of the Son of Man, the day of the coming of Jesus, whereas in Chapter 21, he elaborates on the signs regarding the fall of Jerusalem. However, there seems to be a disparity between these signs and those announcing the end of days and the coming of the Son of Man; the lack of clarity keeps the debate going between exegetes.

The Challenge of Hermeneutics

We must accept the text as it is, since we know that for Luke the fall of the Holy City also meant the end of history. But because things turned out differently, it's up to us to grasp the perennial meaning of the words. This is an example where hermeneutics—the sacred art of interpreting religious texts—faces a real challenge, and we must admit that we still haven't fully understood these passages. Confronted with new events, future generations might well understand them better; for the time being, we shall make an effort to get inside the mind of Jesus and Luke.

What can we make of the eschatological teaching in Luke 21?

The contemplation of the temple, as it appears in the introduction, provides Jesus with the opportunity to intervene: "As some spoke of the temple, how it was adorned with costly stones and gifts . . ." (Lk 21:5). When visiting what remains of the temple, we are impressed by the power they exude and we can easily imagine the fascination the temple of Jerusalem held over its visitors before it was destroyed, with its stones set one upon the other in a perfectly geometric pattern. On the other hand, we have no idea what the votive offerings were like; maybe they resembled our commemorative gifts, silver shields and plaques to recall the temple's own history and all the prayers and expressions of hope connected to those sacred walls.

Jesus starts by saying that all that will fall. It's an explosive statement, unthinkable, almost blasphemous. Indeed, among the charges made against Jesus, we find the words "I shall destroy this temple," which could be a distortion of verse 6: "As for these things which you behold, the days will come in which there shall not be left one stone upon another, that shall not be thrown down." It may sometimes seem blasphemous to even think it, but even great buildings like Milan's Cathedral will come to an end one day! Everything is fragile, impermanent, destined to die. Jesus' predictions frightened the disciples, as a similar fate frightens us. According to the calculations of astrophysicists and nuclear physicists, life on earth will have disappeared in a few million years. The universe is destined to end. Let that be a reminder not to be too attached to this world as if it were the only reality or to the temple as if it were indestructible. What is indestructible lies deeper, beyond mere stones.

However, Jesus' first intervention provides Him with the motive to deliver his speech. Following his comments on the beauty and impermanence of the temple, He is asked two questions: when will it fall and what are the signs? "Master, but when shall these things be? And what signs will there be when these things shall come to pass?" (Lk 21:7). Again, the disciples seem to refer to the destruction of the temple and the fall of Jerusalem. Matthew distinguishes more clearly between the two events, but in fact, Luke's account is more logical because, for the disciples, the destruction of the temple marks the end of all things. Through Jesus' answer—apparently clear, yet very enigmatic—we learn the distinction between the two.

Verses 8-24 relate Jesus' answer, in which He describes the dramatic events leading to the fall of Jerusalem and the days of the Gentiles: "Jerusalem shall be trodden down by Gentiles, until the times of the Gentiles be fulfilled" (Lk 21:24). What does it mean? What does it mean specifically today since there is a new state of Israel? It remains a mystery.

Even if the first answer focuses mainly on Jerusalem, Jesus probably widens its scope and introduces bigger cosmic signs that lead up to the end of the world: "Nation shall rise against nation, and kingdom against kingdom. And great earthquakes shall be in different places, and famines, and pestilences; and fearful sights and great signs shall there be from heaven" (Lk 21:10-11).

Jesus' Exhortation to Vigilance

Jesus' second answer (vv. 25-28) focuses on the ultimate revelation of the Son of Man, in other words, on the end of history. After giving his two answers—one more historical, the other more eschatological—

Jesus tells the parable of the fig tree (vv. 29-33) to introduce the *exhortation to vigilance* that is at the heart of his speech. *Be vigilant*, like he who observes the leaves of the fig tree; *be watchful*, lest at any time your hearts be overwhelmed with excesses, greed, and cares of this life (Lk 21:34-36).

In my opinion, the text is significant for us mainly through these exhortations that begin already in the first part; it is not so much about what future Jesus is referring to, but rather about the attitudes that He wishes us to adopt today.

We have attempted to grasp the structure, the pattern of Jesus' speech; now we must reread more carefully verses 8-11 in order to underline four significant events that Jesus refers to as an expression of the tragic, ambiguous, and impermanent aspects of history.

First of all, false prophets: "Many shall come in my name, saying *I am the one*, and *The time draws near*" (v. 8). These are typical proclamations that Jesus makes: in John's Gospel, the statements "I am the one" and "The time draws near" sum up the preaching of the Son of God. We could say that the false prophets are good imitators. For this reason, Jesus warns his disciples: "Take heed that you be not deceived [. . .] therefore, do not go after them!" (v. 8).

Other premonitory events that show the ambiguity and brevity of history are wars and revolutions. Again, Jesus exhorts us not to fear: "When you shall hear of wars and revolutions, be not terrified: for these things must first come to pass; but the end is not by and by" (v. 9).

Then, there will be uprisings: "Nation shall rise against nation, and kingdom against kingdom" (v. 10) and many dramatic events: great earthquakes, famines, pestilences, fearful sights and great signs from heaven (v. 11).

A Time to Meditate

I would like to suggest four points that I have drawn from reading and meditating on the words of Jesus. Each one of you can then ask in a personal prayer: "Holy Spirit, Spirit of wisdom and intellect, enlighten me so that I can tackle even the difficult verses of the passage from Luke; help me understand what they mean for us today; as we are enveloped in the darkness of history, we cannot see it from above, as You can."

Thanks to Jesus' words, we are certain that, even in a world threatened by chaos and shaken by every kind of catastrophe, God's plan will be achieved. Such a certainty runs through the entire passage. Perhaps today, we understand even more clearly than the philosophers of Antiquity that the world is threatened by chaos; for them, chaos coincided with the natural events of the cosmos. It was interesting to hear from scientists who are non-believers how the origins of the universe were fortuitous: had just a few conditions been different, the universe would be a shapeless, spinning mass, waiting for life to rise (the concept of "waiting" for something to happen is of course totally unscientific). Therefore, the idea of chaos from which everything emerges and which can swallow up everything again is a very central concept to modern science.

Jesus says: it is natural to be afraid; the universe is indeed chaotic, but history has meaning. He thus invites us to hold on to that meaning which is not immanent to history, but goes beyond it.

A second consideration for meditation: in all the synoptic Gospels, the eschatological sayings precede the account of the Passion because what matters in the Gospels is to understand the mystery of Christ on the Cross. Even the text that we have been studying tries to comfort Christians by inviting them to join in the Passion of Christ with the certainty that enemy forces—whatever they may be—will not prevail. History is in God's hands and we can face persecution with confidence. Nothing can hurt us if we remain sons [daughters] of the Son, just as Jesus was the Son in his Passion.

The third point concerns the immanent meaning of history, seen as a body of signs that accompany the ongoing process of salvation; this process moves towards the revelation of the completeness of the Kingdom. The signs ("what will be the signs, when will these things come to pass?") tell us that God reveals his power and foretells it. Thus what is presented is a theological view of history.

A fourth point stems from Luke's text: the exhortations that are woven through the writing. "Take heed that you be not deceived, for many shall come in my name" (Lk 21:8). It is an invitation to be discerning. All kinds of people will try to imitate Christ: gurus, leaders, celebrities will attempt to win over your hearts: "Take heed that you be not deceived," I am the only Lord. It is a very topical exhortation nowadays. "Do not go after them." Don't be fooled by short-term mirages; he who does not propose and accept my primacy is a false prophet.

The second exhortation is also very difficult to follow. "When you shall hear of wars and revolutions, do not be terrified" (Lk 21:9). We get frightened when we hear news of wars and revolutions that happen all over the world. And yet, missionaries do not panic; they show heroic courage; they live and walk in the midst of violence and destruction; they suffer for themselves and their people, but they don't let their fear overcome them, even if they are sometimes tempted to do so. The second exhortation helps us not to be overwhelmed by historical events and to have faith in Jesus' words: "Do not be terrified."

In verses 18-19, we find the third exhortation: "not one hair on your head shall perish. Your patience will save your soul." Christ urges his disciples to let go in the midst of turmoil. It doesn't mean that there will be no suffering and even martyrdom, but that we are in God's hands and we must persevere, have patience (*ypomonè* in Greek), put up a resistance against adversity.

Fostering Hope

Jesus' entire speech asks of us what is essentially the basic attitude of a Christian: knowing how to wait, stand up and bear adversity. It is important for individual lives as well as for pastoral action, which must learn to bear a lot to achieve perfect hope. Patience produces hope (Rom 15:4), creates perfection. Indeed, hope that has not been tested by patience is not hope yet.

We find here the meaning of all hardships: they too are signs that the Lord, who is the master of history, leads all things to their proper end.

Therefore, the images in this text, even though they may seem far-removed from our lives, help us in fact to reflect on the present; they also foster the hope that can overcome the passing of time and make us anticipate the mystery of eternity.

Christian Vigilance

In Mark's Gospel, the last words that Jesus addresses to the crowd are part of what we call the eschatological sayings. After his sermon, Jesus goes to Jerusalem where He is arrested, tried, and executed. But before that, He speaks again to his disciples at their last supper; He expresses himself briefly during his trial and, finally, says a few words on the Cross. Mark's text (13:33-37) is thus a conclusion to the preceding teachings and it also ends with a warning: "Be vigilant."

Take heed, watch and pray, for you don't know the precise moment. It is like a man taking a long journey, who left his house and gave authority to his servants, and to every man his work, and commanded the porter to watch. Therefore, keep watch, for you don't know when the master of the house will return, in the evening or at midnight, at the cock crowing or in the morning; lest coming suddenly, he should find you sleeping. And what I say to you, I say to all: Watch! (Mk 13:33-37).

I intend to examine the theme of vigilance in four steps. First, the reading itself; then, a meditation on the text that raises a few questions; thirdly, some examples of discernment; fourthly, a conclusion.

This passage, complex and well developed, can be divided into six parts: "Be watchful", in the Greek text "Open your eyes;" "Keep watch, for you don't know the precise moment," a twofold fundamental exhortation and the reason for it. Then, a comparison: "It is like a man taking a long journey, who left his house and gave authority to his servants . . . ;" "Therefore, keep watch, for you don't know when the master of the house will return . . . ," in other words, a new exhortation to stay awake at all times; then, the fact that it applies to everyone: "And what I say to you, I say to all"; and the exhortation again as conclusion: "Keep watch."

These verses form Jesus' eschatological discourse, one that relates to the end of an era, specifically in Matthew's Gospel, the end of the world. However, eschatological discourses are not intended to awaken fear or bewilderment, but rather to suggest how to behave in the difficult times of transition, with a view to the great and total transition, the end of history itself. On the other hand, every era has their own critical situations, and it is right that it should be so, so that mankind doesn't get lazy and fall asleep. Jesus teaches us how to act, and the key words are: keep watch, be vigilant, stay awake.

Examining the Terms

It might be useful in this exercise to reflect briefly on the two fundamental verbs used in the passage: "watch" and "be vigilant." A 2003 translation uses two different terms to translate the two Greek words, watching being mainly a physical action and being vigilant, a more spiritual reality. The Greek verbs themselves refer to two fairly different experiences.

The first, translated by "watch" in the sense of "keeping watch" or "being watchful," refers to sleeping outdoors, as a shepherd would; he may be sleeping, but he is always aware of his flock and his surroundings and he keeps his ears open for suspicious sounds—approaching thieves, wolves, whining sheep. The second verb, translated by "be vigilant," expresses the physical experience of waking up in time and resisting falling asleep.

"Watch," which in Greek is literally "open your eyes," "look," poses a problem. What does it mean to "look?" In Mark's Gospel, this exhortation occurs in other important contexts. "Watch (take heed) what you hear" (Mk 4:24), in other words, make sure your eyes are wide open in order to better understand what is being said to you. The same expression comes back as a reproach in chapter 8: “You have eyes, yet do not see; you have ears, yet do not hear” (v. 18) and, in the same context, the point is clarified: “Perceive you not yet, neither understand? Is your heart hardened?” (v. 17) and then once more in verse 21: “How is it that you do not understand?”

Jesus urges us, not so much to look with our physical eyes, but to be perspicacious, to use our intuition, our powers of intellectual penetration and our wisdom to understand events. The two main verbs that open and conclude the passage thus constitute its very framework: keep watch, stay awake all of you, be vigilant.

After having underlined the supporting elements of this passage from the Gospel, we can now go deeper into other interesting aspects of the text; for example, the comparison of the Lord to the master who leaves and can return suddenly. The text clearly suggests shared responsibility in the household. Those who wait for the master to come back are not mere servants, but people who actually look after the house. We are reminded of the parable of the talents and the need to make what we have received work for us and bear fruit. The passage we have been reading is full of significant references and I leave it to your personal reflection.

The Lord’s Coming

Moving on to our meditation on the text, I am eager to raise two questions. The first one concerns the reason for being vigilant: we just don't know the precise moment of the coming of the Lord, the *kairòs* in the Greek text.

What is the time at which the master could arrive and find us asleep? What does the sudden arrival of the Lord mean? In the Scriptures, the coming of God has many different meanings.

First of all, there is an unforeseen "coming" that man attempts to ignore because he doesn't want to know: death. No one escapes death, yet everybody tries to think about it as little as possible. Death is the inexorable coming of a complete transition that affects all human beings and to which Jesus often refers. You surely recall the parable of the rich country landlord who, after a generous harvest, builds new barns and makes all kinds of new plans, when he hears God say to him: "You fool, tonight your soul shall be required of you. And what you have prepared, whose shall those things be?" (Lk 12:20).

In the context of chapter 13 in Mark—and of parallel chapters in the other evangelists—the coming of the Lord is connected with the great historical disasters, which force each person to decide what really matters to them, take a stand, convert. In the same chapter, Mark calls these great events "the beginning of sorrows": "For nation shall rise against nation, kingdom against kingdom; and there shall be earthquakes, famines and troubles. This will be the beginning of sorrows" (Mk 13:8). However, the translation is not clear, because the Greek text says: "This will be the beginning of the pains," the pains of labor.

What we have here is a biblical concept that sees two possible meanings in all devastating events throughout history: one of catastrophe and pain, and one of rebirth and the beginning of a new world.

And this is where the importance of "watching" and "being vigilant" acquires its full significance: we must learn to distinguish between events and adopt the right attitude, so that what happens to us or others is not just a cursed misfortune, a fatal event, but is received in its providential significance, which is that of a transition to and beginning of a new life.

In the context of the history of salvation, trouble and pain bring with them the extraordinary force of hope. The great Italian novelist, Alessandro Manzoni, put it simply: "God would never upset his children, unless He was preparing a greater and more certain joy for them."

He who sees in the troubles of humanity nothing but misfortunes and unhappiness; who blames himself, relatives, friends and society in general, is nothing but a tormented soul. But he who sees in every event an opportunity to renew himself, to understand past errors and redirect his energies, is awake and vigilant.

A third meaning is that of the coming of God upon the entire human adventure, in other words, the end of history. The Bible often speaks of the end in order to survey history and the life of humankind from the point of view of the Lord who completely dominates the unfolding of time. For us, it is difficult to consider time as a unit moving toward the end because we are inside time, but God sees this unit as having a global, organic sense that He will reveal only on the last day. Just as the history of every human being is defined by a biological cycle, so does humanity have its own cycle that will reach a final conclusion.

That will be the definitive coming of God, the eschatological judgment that will allow us to see history from God's point of view. Only then, we, limited beings confined to the obscurity of any single century, will be able to contemplate history as God does.

Finally, God's coming is a daily thing. God comes upon us in every hardship and every joy of our lives, each time we have the opportunity to make an ethical choice. That's because each time, we pass judgment on ourselves, depending on whether we choose light or darkness, life or death; whether we choose with the strength of the Holy Spirit or the impulse of our worldliness.

Therefore, "the precise moment" when the Lord will come is either the moment of great historical transitions, that is, the moment that will allow us to judge the whole of humanity, as well as every ethical moment of our lives.

A second question: what does it mean to keep watch and be vigilant? It means that history is a time for discernment, the time when a Christian is called upon to open his eyes and not let events submerge him purely and simply as fatal occurrences. He is invited to react positively, with intelligence and courage.

Biblical Vigilance

In order for us to understand even better the exhortation to keep watch and be vigilant, we will consider three aspects of biblical vigilance as we find it in the Gospel. First of all, there is the watch the master keeps at night, when he fears a thief might come. This is the watch dictated by prudence, a precaution; it's being very attentive to one's surroundings. Then there is the vigilance of the servant who is waiting for his master's return and is eager to be found fully active at his post; it's the watch dictated by loyalty. Finally, there is the watch kept by the bride waiting for her spouse, as found in the Song of Songs. The woman is waiting for the man she loves: hers is the watch of love, of desire that calls out: "Come, Lord Jesus."

We find these same three aspects of Christian vigilance when we contemplate Jesus during his agony in the Garden of Gethsemane. He keeps watch while his disciples fall asleep, just like the master watching out for the thief, because He wants to be awake when Judas arrives; He keeps watch out of loyalty to the Father whose will He wishes to do, not his own. He keeps watch in love, crying out to the Father that the cup of passion come upon him. In the Garden of Gethsemane, Christ is the perfect model of Christian vigilance, of precaution, loyalty, and love.

We sometimes postpone acting or expressing ourselves until a better day comes, until that time when there will be more justice, more peace and understanding among men. The Gospel reminds us that now is the time to speak and act, for now is the coming of the Lord. Christians must wait attentively for this coming in the midst of the contradictions and contrasts of history.

He who waits for the historical palingenesis waits in vain.

To be watchful means keeping one's eyes open in the night: God comes even when man is at his most negative, as in the event of the Cross. The Cross summarizes perfectly this attitude of watchfulness: man is at his worst and Jesus comes to save him.

What conclusion can we draw from this section of Mark's Gospel?

Let me first remind you of Jesus' words, still from chapter 13: ". . . the sun shall be darkened and the moon shall not give its light, and the stars of heaven shall fall and the powers that are in heaven shall be shaken" (Mk 13:24-25). However, after these catastrophic words, Jesus adds: "And then shall they see the Son of Man coming in the clouds with great power and glory" (Mk 13:26).

What seemed to be a decisive and irrevocable cataclysm becomes an opportunity for contemplating the Son of Man. The corresponding passage in Luke's Gospel is even more moving: "And when these things come to pass, lift up your heads and look up, for your redemption draws near" (Lk 21:28).

In my own words: do not wait for good times to be Christian, for one is Christian precisely at times of historical upheavals, big or small, keeping in mind the criterion of the Cross.

It is human and the result of our fragility to overcome evil with evil, whether it be the evil of violence or that of despair. But overcoming evil with good is divine; in so doing, we proclaim the power of the Cross of Christ. It is in the act of overcoming evil with good that God comes upon us.

Giving Death a Voice

The Church's position on death has always been the same; however, the message needs to be adapted to successive generations and changing times.

The Christian position on death is complex and almost seems contradictory to an outsider: "God didn't create death" says the Book of Wisdom. "He has created all things to be" (. . . 1:13-14). In his first Epistle to the Corinthians, Saint Paul reminds them that "death has entered the world because of man." It is the ultimate enemy, "the last enemy to be annihilated."

The Holy Scriptures teach us something else: that there is a good death, a death that is like a baptism from which life is reborn. Such is Jesus' death: He welcomes it because He finds necessity and meaning in it: ". . . having loved his own who were in the world, he loved them to the end" (Jn 13:1). The expression with which Jesus gives a voice to his own death is repeated every day in the liturgy of the Church. "This is my body which is given up for you." With these words, Jesus gives meaning to his death, and through them, He dissolves its bitterness and remedies its cruelty. The message is sober, humble, patient, unhurried; those who heard it probably did not fully understand it. However, they did not forget it, but rather jealously kept it while waiting for the day when its meaning and promise would be revealed. That day goes on today.

We Christians celebrate the bread and the wine "in memory" of Jesus: that is how we try and understand his legacy and find in the New Testament a message of hope for our own death. The prospect of dying calls upon us, as free individuals, to find the message of hope that will give meaning to our death and make us agree not to rebel in vain against it, as if it were a cruel and senseless fate.

This is the "good death" to which everyone is entitled.

Instead of that, the greatest desire that people have today when facing death is that they or their loved ones be spared all suffering. As a consequence, the humanitarian approach to the dying tends to merely alleviate suffering, be it physical or psychological. When we take that point of view, it is easy to justify euthanasia as a means to accelerate someone's death in order to reduce inevitable suffering for those who are dying and ourselves.

In that sense, euthanasia is a symptom of the loss of hope. Indeed, the only measure of what a human being is capable of enduring is the one set by the hope sustaining him. Therefore, when confronting the ultimate experience of our lives, we must try to nurture hope while attempting to alleviate suffering.

Transmitting Signs of Hope

If the task of giving a more acceptable face and voice to death appears difficult, even impossible to many of our contemporaries, it is probably due to our bad habit of only wanting quick answers and resolutions. We find it hard to say and do things whose impact cannot be measured immediately on the faces or by the responses of those we are addressing. By contrast, words and gestures that evoke feelings and the true meaning of things such as death, can only be delivered patiently, sown like seeds in soil, not cast with bitterness, but rather with the knowledge that they will bear fruit only much later.

I was particularly moved by the story of a terminally ill patient that was used in a recent study on the psychology of death: after speaking to his doctor who came to visit him regularly, the patient offered the doctor his cane as he managed a few unsteady steps along the corridors of the hospital. The doctor tried to dissuade him, assuring him that he would need his cane for a while yet. But the patient insisted and the doctor finally accepted. The next day, she learned that he had died during the night. That cane, a silent legacy that was offered and initially refused, started to speak in a language of its own, clearer, more eloquent and poignant only after the event.

It's not always easy to recognize this type of indirect communication, but they can ease the intense emotions that prevent us from giving a voice to imminent death. This is especially true of persons with strong family ties. In those cases, we must frankly acknowledge that it's practically impossible to find such persuasive signs. They will be given to us only if we fervently hope that death will not have the last word in our life.

And that is precisely the goal of the Church's pastoral care: announcing a hope beyond death and, at the same time, giving human beings the signs, the sacraments through which they can articulate and live that hope. In carrying out this duty, the Church has a clear advantage thanks to its deeper knowledge of the empirical modalities of dying today—medical and psychological modalities, modalities shaped by culture and historical evolution—and also to its intuitive perception of art and philosophy.

In conclusion, I would like to suggest two excerpts to ponder.

The first comes from "Memorial to the Citizens of Milan" (*Memoriale ai milanesi*) written by Saint Charles Borromeo. He dedicated this Memorial to his "beloved citizens of Milan" after the plague had devastated their city, to urge them to reflect on the meaning of what had happened. From that very long text, I shall only quote a few lines.

The Death of Civilizations

Saint Charles describes death in the city by referring to the biblical image of the death of the tree in

King Nebuchadnezzar's dream: in it, the king saw a big tree that all of a sudden fell with all its leaves and fruit. Saint Charles writes:

> Oh city of Milan, your greatness rose to the sky, your riches extended to the ends of the earth. People, animals, birds lived and fed from your abundance. Then all of a sudden, pestilence comes from heaven, and you become an object of contempt in the eyes of the world. You are confined behind your walls, your goods are locked in behind your borders; no one comes to live inside you, to feed upon your fruits. Your great citizens fled, and so did the little people; so many abandoned you, noblemen and commoners alike. And you, Milan, city in distress, in constant need of being assisted by cities, castles and poor villages all around, you were astonished, in disbelief, totally stunned!

The theme that Saint Charles develops at length in his *Memorial* is clear: not only can individuals die, but the entire civilization is at risk of declining and dying if it doesn't keep going back to its original ideals. In this tragic "if," we can read the powerful conditionals in which so many catastrophic prophecies are regularly made by prophets and seers on the fate of contemporary civilizations. Today more than ever, so-called doomsayers proliferate! Educated people smile at such prophecies, yet they are in part tragically serious. They actually express a very simple truth: if the promise of supernatural salvation for human beings does indeed exist, it does not for civilizations. They will be saved or damned, that is, they will deteriorate and decline, depending on a number of "ifs" and conditions that relate to their moral purity.

History reminds us that often civilizations do not pass the test: Babylonia dies, Niniveh dies, so do Sodom and Gomorrah, Tyre and Sidon.

What I mean is that reflecting on the death of civilizations is a cultural duty, somehow even more urgent than reflecting on the death of individuals. At any rate, the two are linked, because if the individual dies of drugs, the civilization is dragged down with him.

The plague described by Saint Charles is sometimes a symbol for plagues that threaten the life of our cities and against which we must defend ourselves with all our might, since we can be assured of our salvation only if we make a strong moral commitment.

A Thought for Life

The second excerpt I wish to quote comes from one of the most beautiful texts by Pope Paul VI, a text that comforts the heart and the spirit. It is entitled "A Thought for Death," but in fact, it is a thought for life. It dates back to the last years of Montini's pontificate; he kept it secret and it was published one year after his death. The entire text is magnificent because it shows us how to face death with an attitude of obedience. In the excerpt I have chosen, the Pope speaks to God and exclaims:

> Here I am at your service, at your love. Here I am in a sublimated state that does not allow me to fall back into the instinctive psychology of a simple man, except to remind myself of what I am and react with infinite trust by giving the answer that I must: amen, *fiat: Tu sciat quia amo Te*, let it be, let it be. You know that I love You. A state of tension sets into a permanent act of absolute faithfulness my will to serve out of love: *in finem dilexit*, he loved until the end. Don't let me be separated from You. The sunset of our lives, which we would like to be restful and serene, must instead be an ever-growing effort toward vigilance, dedication and waiting. It is difficult, but that is how death seals the destination of our earthly pilgrimage and bridges our way to the great reunion with Christ in eternal life. I gather my remaining strength and do not shrink away from the total gift of myself, as I think of yours: *consummatum est*, all is completed.

It seems to me that these words express well the fact that we can look death in the face after a life intensely lived, full of emotions, a life never denied, but profoundly loved, a life brought to the ultimate gift of oneself.

The Experience of the Risen Christ in Daily Life

Our great feast, the feast of all Christians, the feast of the Church, of life, the feast of victory over death: that is Easter.

But what do we mean by these expressions? What should we do to make sure that the joy of Easter, which we feel in our hearts, is not superficial, fragile, inconsistent?

The episode in the Gospel that tells us of Mary Magdalen by the sepulchre can help us to grasp the meaning of the mystery of the Resurrection.

> But Mary stood outside the sepulchre weeping, and as she wept, she stooped down and looked into the sepulchre; and she saw two angels in white, sitting, the one at the head and the other at the feet, where the body of Jesus had been laid. And they said to her: Woman, why are you weeping? She answered: Because they have taken away my Lord, and I know not where they have laid him. And when she had said this, she turned around and saw Jesus standing, but did not know that it was Jesus. Jesus said to her: Woman, why are you weeping? Whom do you seek? Supposing him to be the gardener, she said: Sir, if you have taken him away, tell me where you have laid him, and I shall go and fetch him. Jesus said to her: Mary! She turned around and said *Rabboni*, which is to say Master! Jesus said to her: Do not touch me, for I am not yet ascended to my Father, but go to my brethren and say to them, I ascend to my Father, and your Father, and to my God, and your God. Mary Magdalen came and told the disciples that she had seen the

Lord, and that he had spoken these things to her. —Jn 20:11-18

It is interesting that Mary's crying is mentioned four times: she stands outside the sepulchre and cries; as she cries, she stoops down; the angels ask her the reason for her crying and so does Jesus: Why are you crying?

Her crying sums up the crying of humankind in the face of death; it sums up the dismay, the distress, the grief, the internal fracture that man feels when confronted with the victory of the sepulchre over life, of evil over good, of darkness over light, of injustice over justice, of lying over truth.

Mary's crying is a legitimate one; it is heart-breaking, without hope: she sees in the sepulchre the end of a friend's life. That's why she contemplates it as if it were the last reality she can take in, a closed, definitive reality that leaves no room for the good tidings from God.

Seeing Eternity in the Now

And as long as we cry with Mary and remain sad, we cannot see anything but the sepulchre, we can't even recognize the Risen Christ Who is standing right next to us.

Such is the human condition. Man goes towards his own death and he knows about it from the start. The thought of death gnaws away at him throughout his life, contrary to animals who sense death only when it is threatened or imminent. We could actually say that the certainty of death is the beginning of our dying. We inevitably exist in relation to the end; we see our life as a succession of specific periods of time that move towards an irrevocable deadline. Indeed, contemporary philosophy speaks of an "existence destined for death."

We can dismiss the thought of death, we can exorcise it, we can accept or refuse it. Whatever we do, we are taking a stand. It is difficult not to raise the question of what happens to us after death. What will become of all the riches that constituted our life, such as love, loyalty, grief, friendship, responsibility, freedom, conscience, service? Indeed, we sense that these things are of a different nature from the biological world.

The Christian answer to these questions confirms our feeling, but it does not simply say that those riches will remain and that after death, we shall continue to live. Rather, it says that, with Christ's resurrection, eternity is already here; the new and definitive life has already become, here and now, part of my experience. The new life comes from placing myself in Jesus' hands, Jesus who died and resurrected, from placing myself in the hands of the Father as Jesus did. This way, the eternity of Jesus Who won over death enters in me and becomes part of my life as of now. The thought of my physical death is not dismissed, but rather sublimated and transfigured by the certainty that eternal life is part of today's experience; I live now in Jesus' eternity, in his glorious, definitive life; He is in me and I am with the Father Who has been and will be forever.

I experience this every time I carry out an act of faith and love; every time I receive the Eucharist or another sacrament; every time I make a good, serious, ethically relevant decision. I experience eternity; I have internalized it thanks to the Risen Christ Who is within me.

The experience of eternity is implicit, by the grace of the Risen Christ, in every free moral act, in every action we carry out, not for our own convenience, but because it is right, true, even if it goes against our interest.

Every time we do an ethically good thing, we participate in God's gift to us of his eternal Being, of his being an eternally true and just God, good in the absolute, of having shown Himself as such in the truth, loyalty, love and justice of Jesus.

And so, the Resurrection is close to us, eternity is within us, and Jesus gives us life; the Holy Spirit lives within us, the Father calls out to us that we are his children and that we can invoke him as our Father.

Mary Magdalen cries because she fears death, because she is overwhelmed by the thought that the One she loves is dead. Mary Magdalen is seeking life, resurrection for herself and others. And Jesus calls her by name: "Mary!" He does not utter arguments or explanations, only her name, spoken with love. The voice reveals the mystery. On hearing that voice, Mary turns toward Jesus; she forgets about the sepulchre and her own past. Each one of us will be freed from the past, from all that enslaves us, from our neuroses, from our inability to express ourselves. After saying to Jesus: I am seeking life and resurrection in You, we will be called by name in our Baptism, our Confirmation, the Eucharist, in the prayer and the joy of Easter.

Jesus calls us by name in the fullness of life and we want to proclaim with Mary: *Rabboni*, Master, my Lord, You Who give me everything, Who are the Lord of the Church and history, You Who will never fail us, Who put eternity in our lives as of now.

And Jesus calls out to Mary: "Go to your brethren," go tell them the news. When Jesus calls us brother, sister, we feel the joy of telling everyone that we are God's children, that each gesture of love brings eternity in our midst. We no longer fear death, for life reigns supreme in every authentic act of love and truth.

This is the Easter message: I have seen the Lord, I have felt his presence; I know that I live with Him, that nothing can make me despair of the future. I know because He is already part of my life every time I perform an act of goodness, truth, loyalty and justice towards others.

The Lord has come upon us. The joy of Easter consists in letting the transforming power of the Spirit of the Risen Christ take hold of us; He opens our eyes and shows us that the tomb is empty, that the world has opened up to let in God's life and that there is in our hearts a place where eternity grows in the simplicity of daily life. Everyone can participate in the eternity of

Christ who shines today in the life of the Church and the life of each one of us.

"I have seen the Lord, and He called us all brothers [sisters]:" from this message stems the Church's missionary role. It is not a form of proselytizing that aims at increasing the number of people baptized or its own glory, but rather a joyful spreading, gratuitous and unselfish, of the gift the Church has received: the Risen Christ.

Let us ask Mary, mother of Jesus, who was the first to experience such joy, to make us share in it.

3
Inside the Mystery

How Chronos Devours His Children

THE way in which a Christian relates to time appears paradoxical at first sight: on the one hand, time is something precious, something dense, full, and on the other hand, something relative and light. It makes me think of Angelo Silesius' provocative statement: "Time is nobler than a thousand eternities." An enigmatic expression, indeed, but one that brings out the fact that, for a Christian, time is the fragile and precarious place in which he determines his own eternity.

The Christian concept of time is already strongly present in the New Testament through the relationship that is established between eschatology and salvation, between the closure of time that comes with God's judgment and the full meaning of the present moment. This concept is underlined incisively in the *Letter to Diognetus*, from the second century A.D., which reminds us that Christ's disciples live in their time, but are already citizens of eternal time: "Christians live in cities inhabited by Greeks and barbarians [. . .], they adapt to the local customs in food, clothing and any other way of life [. . .]. Any foreign land becomes their homeland, yet every homeland remains a foreign land. They dwell on earth, but are citizens of heaven."

I shall now review the objections and temptations inside me with regard to such an exacting dimension of time, in order to answer the question: how does Chronos attempt to devour his children? A certain perception of time, possibly implicit and unconscious, underlies each one of these temptations. These are numerous, but I will define only a few: the time of anxiety, the time of frustration, time that repeats itself, the time of closure.

Four Concepts of Time

First, the most common, the one that is easily perceived as a disease, is anxiety: there never is enough time and there are so many things to do. Very often, to get out of a commitment, we put forward as an excuse or a pretext that we don't have the time: I can't make it; I don't even have time to breathe. The French philosopher Michel Serres puts it quite well: "Everybody has a watch and nobody has time. Exchange one for the other: leave your watch and take back your time." But who has the courage to do that?

A second temptation or excess is the time of frustration: time flies, it disintegrates in our hands; we fall into depression or "acedia"—in the language of the hermit—or, at the other extreme, we are dying to do things, we are overwhelmed by passion, greed, competitiveness, possessiveness, and the thirst for power. What is behind these attitudes is precisely the obscure perception of time's finiteness, of the specter of death as the inexorable end of all possibilities.

There is an even more serious temptation: the temptation of time repeating itself, of cloned time, so to speak. It stems from the fear of a definitive rendering of accounts, the fear of reaching the end of the line without the possibility of further appeals. This fear makes the doctrine of reincarnation very attractive, which explains its renewed popularity in the West. Reincarnation gives the impression that we have one more chance, that we can put off fundamental decisions until our next life and that we don't have to make choices for all eternity. It is certainly easier and it involves no commitment if we think of our life without having to make any definitive and irrevocable decisions. It implies a cyclical concept of time, symbolized by the snake biting its tail. This is the myth of the eternal recurrence of what has been.

Just as serious is the temptation of time that ends or is denied: premised on the belief that there is nothing beyond physical life or above man, the future is reduced to the visible limits of biological time. From this narrow view comes the claim to the right to control one's own life and, in specific circumstances, to plan one's death.

These and other temptations correspond to the different views on the meaning of time. Each one of us, even if we are not aware of it, has a concept of time that expresses a certain concept of life.

Time in Scripture

To these questions about time, I will answer as a believer. Obviously, my guide is the Gospel, in particular a word which recurs four times in the Gospel according to Luke in extraordinarily dense situations. It is the word "today": when I compare my position to the different concepts of time, four perceptions come to mind. I will present them, then compare them to the texts in the Gospel.

First, the perception that time is brief, that time flies: today seems little more than an instant, the days and the seasons come and go in rapid succession. Everything passes incredibly fast and I find myself repeating with everyone else: I need more time; I wish I had more time. Today is fleeting, always precarious.

And yet, it seems to me that today is full: the here and now is rich in substance. Every moment has its significance; it sends out a message that reaches eternity.

I both know and sense that time will end, and the end will bring a judgment: there will finally come a moment, a definitive today when I will find out, without hypocrisy or illusions, what meaning my actions had, if I acted well or badly during my life.

I therefore understand that eternity is already part of time. There is an event which, if viewed in a linear, not cyclical, concept of temporality, has irrevocably marked time starting from something that is outside time.

I do not intend to take up again the four perceptions of time in a simplistic presentation. I would rather refer to the four passages in the Gospel according to Luke that contain the word "today," the key word in directing my understanding of time. We find it for the first time in chapter 2, when the birth in Bethlehem is announced to the shepherds: ". . . I bring you good tidings of great joy, which shall be to all people. For unto you is born today in the city of David a Savior [. . .] You shall find the baby wrapped in swaddling clothes . . ." (Lk 2:10-12). In this passage, "today" indicates the density of the present to which the future is subordinated (the "great joy which shall be to all people"), and the future stems from a promise made in the past by Isaiah (Isa 9:5): "For unto us a child is born, unto us a son is given."

Therefore, there is a dense and decisive "today" that recalls the past and promises a future. This brings to mind the pregnant sentence by T. S. Eliot in choruses from "The Rock:" ". . . for without the meaning, there is no time, / and that moment of time gave the meaning." This "today," rich with memory and promise, is found again in Jesus' first public remark, in a sermon He gave in the synagogue in Nazareth. After having read from Isaiah's scroll: "The Spirit of the Lord is upon me [. . .] and he has sent me to bring the glad tidings to the poor." Jesus proclaims: "*Today* is this scripture fulfilled in your ears" (Lk 4:18-21). Again, "today" as fulfillment of the prophecy is the answer to a promise made in the past and opening up onto the future.

A third "today," full of meaning, appears at the moment when Jesus enters the home of Zacchaeus, the tax collector: "*Today* is salvation come to this house, for he is also a son of Abraham." This event is rooted in the past (Abraham is recalled) and points to the work of salvation in the future: "The Son of man is come to seek and save that which was lost" (Lk 19:9-10).

Finally, the "today" Jesus proclaims from the Cross to the thief who was also crucified takes on an even deeper meaning. When he asks: "Lord, remember me when you come into your kingdom," Jesus answers: "Amen, I say to you, today you shall be with me in paradise" (Lk 23:42-43). "Today" opens the door to a fullness without end and such fullness is given by compassion, forgiveness, and love. This "today" is neither frantic nor fleeting, but rather sealed by lasting values, by eternity, by an alliance of ages that transforms the here and now into the present day of salvation.

Christological Foundation

The fullness of the present meets the expectations of the past and opens up perspectives of an endless future. It explains, effectively and concretely, the meaning of time for those who recognize in Jesus Christ time as a whole and the center of history. In the "today," finite and infinite time are not opposites anymore, they do not annul each other, but touch and fuse together.

Without a doubt, I realize more and more that my concept of time is christological; its reference is Jesus Christ Who was made man, was crucified, died and resurrected; Jesus, Lord of history and thus of today.

I have realized that my concept of time refers to the words of the Gospel, spoken and written in the past, and yet current today, because they were spoken about the Holy Spirit's "today." In other words, I am aware that my concept of time is marked by revelation and the workings of God in history through Jesus, his Word, his life.

I wonder whether many people recognize Jesus as the center of history. Probably not. However, a tradition in Western society is worthy of note: we calculate the years starting with the birth of Christ (A.D.—*Annum Domini*), a system introduced by the monk Dionysius in the 6th century; and backwards, the years before Christ, a modern tradition. It is interesting that, by doing that practically everywhere in the world, we underline the central position of Christ in history, which is itself at the root of the Christian concept of time.

I would like to conclude my reflections by alluding to an icon, the story of Jacob's ladder. We read in *Genesis* that Jacob, who was a fugitive in exile, fell asleep in a lonely place, his head resting on a stone, and had a dream:

> And Jacob went out from Beersheba, and went toward Haran. And he came upon a certain place, and tarried there all night, because the sun was set; and he took the stones of that place, and put them under his head, and lay down in that place to sleep. And he dreamed, and behold a ladder set up on the earth, and the top of it reached to heaven:

and behold the angels of God ascending and descending on it. And, behold, the Lord stood above it, and said, I am the Lord God of Abraham your father, and the God of Isaac: the land on which you are lying, to you will I give it, and to your seed. And your seed shall be as the dust of the earth, and you shall spread abroad to the west, and to the east, and to the north, and to the south: and in you and in your seed shall all the families of the earth be blessed. And, behold, I am with you, and will keep you in all places wherever you go, and will bring you again into this land; for I will not leave you, until I have done that which I have spoken to you of.

And Jacob awoke from his sleep, and he said, 'Surely the Lord is in this place; and I knew it not. And he was afraid, and said,' How dreadful is this place! This is none other but the house of God, and this is the gate of heaven. And Jacob rose up early in the morning, and took the stone that he had put under his head, and set it up for a pillar, and poured oil upon the top of it. And he called the name of that place Bethel: but the name of that city was first called Luz.

And Jacob vowed a vow, saying, 'If God will be with me, and will keep me in this way that I go, and will give me bread to eat, and clothes to put on, so that I come again to my father's house in peace; then shall the Lord

> be my God. And this stone, which I have set for a pillar, shall be God's house: and of all that you shall give me I will surely give a tenth to you. —Gen 28:10-22

A ladder linked heaven to earth, and on that ladder angels went up and down. Going from his dream to reality, Jacob understood that he was not alone and abandoned as he thought, and that it was for him a time of hope, not despair. He had been in the grip of fear, feeling like a pilgrim lost in a world without points of reference. And now, the alienating space-time coordinates were transformed into the awareness of the relationship between human destiny and its meaning, which is outside time and space. And so that morning, with renewed courage, he resumed his journey towards his destination.

May we find, like Jacob, in the labyrinth of time, directions to a safe path.

The People's Journey Toward the Light

I would now like to suggest reading an eschatological poem taken from the Book of Isaiah. It is about the last days and it is dominated by the image of light. It could easily be entitled "hymn to the coming light" or "hymn to the peoples' light." It begins with the exhortation: "Arise, shine."

> "Arise, shine, for your light has come,
> and the glory of the Lord rises upon you.
> See, darkness covers the earth
> and thick darkness is over the peoples,
> but the Lord shines upon you

and his glory appears over you.
Nations will come to your light,
and kings to the brightness of your dawn.
Lift up your eyes and look about you:
all assemble and come to you.
Your sons come from afar,
and your daughters are carried on the arm.
Then you will look and be radiant,
your heart will throb and swell with joy;
the wealth on the seas will be brought to you,
to you the riches of the nations will come.
Herds of camels will cover your land,
young camels of Midian and Ephah.
And all from Sheba will come,
bearing gold and incense
and proclaiming the praise of the Lord.

—Isa 60:1-6

Be Light

"Shine," be light: what causes this radiance?

The image of light is found four times in the poem: "for your light has come;" "the glory of the Lord rises upon you"; "the Lord shines upon you"; "his glory appears over you." Hence, the cause of our radiance, of our becoming shining light, is the coming of the Lord upon us; the light comes from Him.

After exhorting us to shine, "to become light," and after using the motif of light, Isaiah describes the result of the Lord's coming upon men: "Nations will come to your light/and kings to the brightness of your dawn." The people are walking in the light while darkness and a thick fog is all around them.

In the pressing invitation that Isaiah illustrates and motivates through its effects, we can see a historical process in four periods: the time of darkness, the time of light from the coming of the Lord, the time to shine, to become light; the time for the people to journey toward the light.

The rest of the excerpt—and of the entire chapter 60 of the Book of Isaiah—from verse 4: "Lift up your eyes and look about you," describe the peoples' procession toward the light, toward the Lord.

This part of the Book of Isaiah raises a few questions and prompts certain remarks.

To whom is the exhortation to shine and the rest of the passage addressed? To Jerusalem, not in the hard times when the prophecy was made, but in the future, the Jerusalem that is hoped for, more glorious than the city of David ever was, more beautiful than the Jerusalem that was rebuilt after the peoples' exile in Babylon.

What event brings the light? It is the coming of the Lord, of the Kingdom of God, the Incarnation of Jesus. On Christmas night, we proclaim: "And the light shines in the darkness [. . . .] That was the true Light, which lights every man that comes into the world" (Jn 1:5-9). The event of the Incarnation is made present, is shown, revealed (epiphany means precisely that, "revelation") in so many other episodes of the life of Jesus, which are remembered in the liturgy: the revelation to the Magi, Jesus' baptism in the Jordan, when a voice from heaven calls him "Son;" the transformation of water into wine at Cana, the multiplication of bread and fish. All these events show the pervasive and transforming power of the light that came over the world and lit up the city of God's children.

This city shining with God's light is the city of the Kingdom, the assembly of those who accept Jesus' criteria for their lives and who place themselves in his hands for grace and forgiveness; it is the community of the Kingdom seen in its eternal fullness, but already started here on earth. Therefore, we are the ones to whom the exhortation is addressed: "Shine, be the light!" But what then is the procession of peoples toward the light? It is the conversion that is happening gradually in the world through the light of God's Kingdom; it is the light radiating from the community that lives according to the values of the Kingdom. This conversion will be complete when all the people are reunited with God for all eternity.

What lesson can we draw from this text? Where is the procession of the peoples happening now?

Everything is fulfilled in the mystery of the Magi in Bethlehem: the light came upon the darkness of the world and shone forth so that great men from afar walked in its splendor to find Jesus; they brought Him gifts of gold, incense and myrrh, and proclaimed the glory of the Lord.

The light has already appeared, and yet it is still ahead; it is God's future that attracts to itself all of history, moment by moment. As a consequence, the mystery is fulfilled every time the Spirit illuminates human reality with Christ's light—an individual existence, a family, a community—until the eternal fullness is achieved.

Isaiah's message thus invites us to view with trust the historical process in which we live. Indeed, we can find in it the same four stages that we have found in the biblical text.

First, the time of darkness and fog. It certainly applies to our times, not just physically, but culturally and spiritually. In chapter 59, Isaiah says: "We wait for light, but behold obscurity; for brightness, but we walk in darkness. We grope for the wall like the blind, and we grope as if we had no eyes" (Isa 59: 9-10).

The Lord comes in the darkness that the prophet foresaw and that we have experienced ourselves. He comes today in his Word, in his Eucharist, in the grace of the Holy Spirit. He comes and illuminates anyone who lets the light in. He comes now and will always come.

We are among those who wish to be illuminated, to accept as true the meaning of existence that Jesus communicates to us through his life and teachings, starting with the humility and simplicity of Bethlehem. The exhortation to "become light" is meant for us too, for the Church, for each one of our families, for each one of our lives: "Arise, shine!"

Every day, many go towards the light because ordinary people bear witness to it in their lives: a priest, a deacon, a religious person, a married couple, a Christian family, even a hidden or silent witness to the Gospel.

"Lift up your eyes and look about you," repeat the Holy Scriptures, and you will see a vast number of small sources of light everywhere and people being illuminated.

The exhortation to look has a missionary relevance, in particular today. It makes us see how, everywhere missionaries go, people are attracted to the light. The sentence resonates for me, too, who was consecrated as a bishop on January 6, 1980. John Paul II laid the book of the Gospels on my head and ordained me as Bishop of the Church of Milan. In his homily, he spoke of the episcopate as the sacrament "of the streets": the bishop sees the streets all lit up with the light of the holy city, and on these streets walk the throngs seeking the light of the Lord. For many years now, I have seen so many people who made the decision to walk toward the light of Jerusalem!

On January 6, 1964, from the cave of Bethlehem, Pope Paul VI spoke to "all those who see Christianity from the outside, as if they were or felt like strangers." One could say, in reference to Isaiah's text, that he spoke to all those who were far from the light that emanates from Jerusalem. He said: "We wish to work for the good of the world, in its real interest, for its salvation. Indeed, we think that the salvation that we offer the world is necessary to it [. . .]. Christianity's mission is one of friendship among the peoples of earth, a mission of understanding, encouragement, advancement, elevation."

That's how Paul VI interpreted the words of the prophet Isaiah and the image of the light that makes Jerusalem shine for all peoples. I feel that the Pope's words also define that part of the mission that commits all of us to those who are not yet walking in full light. For them, we must let the Lord illuminate us; let Him transform our lives and make them, no matter how insignificant, shine for others. That will be the greatest reward for our efforts.

The Final Judgment

I would like to suggest for your meditation an excerpt from Matthew's Gospel on the final judgment. But first, a prayer to the Lord: "We pray, O Lord, that we should understand these words without trying to deny them. We ask that we may know them by our own experience; that we do not only meditate on them, but that we be open to the changes they imply in our lives. You, O Lord, who send the Spirit and live and reign in the beginning, now, and ever more. Amen.

> 31 But when the Son of man shall come in
> his glory, and all the angels with him, he
> shall sit on the throne of his glory: 32 and be-
> fore him shall be gathered all the nations:
> and he shall separate them one from another,
> as the shepherd separates the sheep from the
> goats; 33 and he shall set the sheep on his
> right hand, but the goats on the left. 34 Then

the King shall say to them on his right hand,
"Come, you blessed of my Father, inherit the
kingdom prepared for you from the founda-
tion of the world: 35 for I was hungry, and you
gave me to eat; I was thirsty, and you gave me
drink; I was a stranger, and you took me in;
36 naked, and you clothed me; I was sick, and
you visited me; I was in prison, and you came
to me." 37 Then the righteous shall answer
him, saying, "Lord, when did we see you hun-
gry, and feed you? or thirsty, and give you
drink? 38 And when did we see you a stranger,
and took you in? or naked, and clothed you?
39 And when did we see you sick, or in prison,
and visited you?" 40 And the King shall an-
swer and say to them, "Amen I say to you,
inasmuch as you did it to one of these my
brethren, even these least, you did it to me."
41 Then he shall say to those on his left, "De-
part from me, you cursed, into the eternal fire
which is prepared for the devil and his an-
gels: 42 for I was hungry, and you did not give
me to eat; I was thirsty, and you gave me no
drink; 43 I was a stranger, and you did not
take me in; naked, and you did not clothe me;
sick, and in prison, and you did not visit me."
44 Then they shall answer, saying, "Lord,
when did we see you hungry, or thirsty, or a
stranger, or naked, or sick, or in prison, and
did not minister to you?" 45 Then he shall an-
swer them, saying, "Amen I say to you, inas-

> much as you did it not to one of these least, you did it not to me." 46 And these shall go away into eternal punishment: but the righteous into eternal life. —Mt 25:31-46

I must admit that this passage has been troubling me for a while. Part of me tries to deny it, because I can see it requires certain choices that I may be unable to make. But I must question myself and face the crisis: that's probably why, up until now, I never suggested this passage for meditation.

Let us try and understand together the meaning of this excerpt, all the time keeping in mind that we must not dwell only on one aspect or another. We must try and see, in all honesty before God, in what direction it points us, what it doesn't say and how it helps us to understand the Gospel as a whole.

Correct Interpretation

The passage doesn't say anything directly about the importance of knowing God; in other words, it doesn't answer the question of whether salvation is possible without knowing God: the problem lies outside the direct teaching it aims to give. Nor does it claim to be a complete catalogue of all the works subjected to judgment. It's as if the only ones were works of corporal mercy, notwithstanding all the other pages from Matthew's Gospel in which he recommends mercy, forgiveness, silent and private prayer. Therefore, it would be a mistake to draw from this text a sort of exclusive list of things to do to be saved, which would boil down to works of corporal mercy. The passage is bold, but as happens with many biblical texts, it must be read symbolically, paying attention to the deeper meaning and not giving too much importance to one aspect over another.

Therefore, I suggest it for your meditation without trying to explain it too much; we must try and understand it gradually, precisely because it is difficult, approaching it like the *Principle and Foundation* by Saint Ignatius: we first simply place the text before our eyes and then we reflect on it.

This way, the passage will serve as background for our meditation. I will proceed only to a brief literary analysis of its structure in order to better understand it, as well as its overall teachings. These are not subject to exegetic opinions, and are therefore to be received as fundamental teachings. Finally, I will suggest a point of view, a "place" from which to pray. I only wish to get you started on your reflection, not give you explanations nor draw conclusions, but let the Spirit work within us all.

I think the structure of the passage is quite clear. It begins with a silent action: the Son of Man comes, sits on the throne of his glory and all the people assemble before Him. It seems very likely to me that the correct interpretation refers to all men, not just pagans or Christians, but the whole of humanity after the Gospel has been preached to everyone: it is a judgment on man.

All men are assembled before Him and a silent, enigmatic action takes place: the Son of Man separates, like a shepherd, the sheep from the goats, placing the goats on the left and the sheep on the right. This division of humanity is an enigma.

Why does the King act like a shepherd, why does He divide mankind into two groups? We have always considered humanity as a whole: why does He divide us before God? Humanity means all the individual persons, not the peoples and races.

Exegetes remind us that this initial action corresponds to the actual life of shepherds. It seems that shepherds do indeed separate the goats from the sheep in the evening: goats are vulnerable to the cold and must find shelter at night, whereas sheep like the open air. So, a simple fact from real life becomes a symbol.

The second part of the scene is symmetrical and takes the form of a dialogue. First, on the right, the verb is in the imperative mood: "Come"; this is followed by an explanation of the command: "I was hungry and you gave me something to eat," and the final answer: "Every time you did this to the smallest of my brothers, you did it to me." The scene on the left is perfectly symmetrical: the imperative, the explanation, the question, the answer. As you can see, the whole is constructed with great symmetry and the accent is on the two endings: "Every time you did this, you did it to me."

The Crucial Relationship

The lesson is also contained in the final questions, not in the preceding ones that merely serve to create dramatic tension and thus sustain interest, so that the enigma moves toward the outcome. What is important in the parable is not so much ignorance, but the final reason. The entire scene aims at communicating a fundamental truth: the relationship of man with the Son of Man depends on the relationship of man with man. I believe this to be the decisive element, the final judgment of the story, even though it is presented with theatrical and metaphysical visual elements.

Before such a truth, we must pray: the relationship between man and the Son of Man, which is the crucial relationship in the Gospel, hinges on the history of the relationship between men. Some men have a special relationship with the Son of Man, for example lowly persons; no matter how we see them in the parable, there is a special link between recognizing the Son of Man and recognizing the lowly, working to promote them and those who are last. Generally speaking, one can say that our relationship with God and our relationship with our neighbor are connected: one depends on the other.

At this point, many questions can arise, and indeed exegetes ask them: why this special relationship between the Son of Man and the lowly? Who are they? The weak, the poor in general, simple Christians, or Christians in general, because they appear lowly, poor, persecuted in comparison to the wealthy of the world? Or those who serve the community, the little people who, if recognized as such, make good the relationship with God? This second interpretation is based on the fact that Jesus said: "Let him who wishes to be the greatest be like the smallest; let him who commands be like him who serves," in other words, he who recognizes me in him who serves, he who honors his superiors in the community honors Christ. That is a possible interpretation.

However, I do not think that we have to decide for one or the other, even if today, the more general interpretation seems the most likely: the lowly are the poor in every sense of the word. And even then, if we broaden the concept, it is everyone because Jesus says: "When you do this to even one of these," it seems to me that He is talking about a specific case: you never shrank away from this relationship; even when the situation seemed insignificant to you, precarious, negligible, you were there before Me.

So I believe that, behind this clarification, there is a particular relationship of the lowly and poor with God. These two spheres are bound and indivisible. Jesus does not mean that the relationship with God does not matter and that only the one between men does, but that the two depend on each other. Therefore, his teaching is not aimed at horizontal relationships alone: He says that the foundation of man is God's design for him, his relationship with God, which hinges on the relationship with his neighbor.

If we suppose that the lowly are the poor whom the world despises, exegetes ask themselves why Jesus identifies with them. Perhaps because Jesus himself was poor and despised; the identification is thus historical. Or because God, in his greatness, chooses the poor precisely because He is great. They are, as you can see, different motivations, but the important thing is that it is God's will revealing itself; we must receive and welcome with an open mind, rather than explain, what is revealed, and ask, in faith and prayer, that He make us understand and accept his revelation.

I suggest that in your meditation you look at this reality without trying to dissect it in all its consequences, and that you say: "O Lord, make me understand how this reality can change my life even a little."

Take an Honest Look

Let us ask ourselves and the Lord what is our place in the scene of the judgment. I will make some hypotheses. I can place myself outside the scene and consider it from there. We wonder who the poor are, who are all the people, what Jesus is trying to tell us, what is the meaning of the question. Does "We have recognized You?" suppose real ignorance or is it just a surprise effect? We could speculate on the parable forever.

Or we can place ourselves inside the scene. That is the first choice we have to make: whether to look at it from the inside or from the outside. If the Lord inspires us to place ourselves inside, we will ask: "O Lord, where shall I stand? Shall I join the poor who are waiting for someone to do something for them? I could say: I am like them and I am waiting; I thank

You, Lord, for placing me among the poor, so that my brother, by accepting and loving me, accepts You. It would be wonderful: we could praise the Lord for making each one of us one of his poor for we have truly given ourselves to others and the Church. We can be sure of that because, even if He seems to have abandoned us, the Lord has put us in the hands of our neighbor and has given his guarantee.

So I place myself among the poor and I thank Him: "O Lord, I thank You because I don't need to be accepted by others; You yourself defend my cause, You yourself sustain me. I can take pride in my poverty, like Saint Paul; I can take pride in my being a not too competent, not too influential person, often slower than my brothers, because You are with me and my cause is your cause.

"Or I can join the righteous and say: 'I thank You, Lord, because You grant me to live my life in the service of my brothers, in a real relationship with You. I thank You for everything in my life that is tiring, that seems useless or requires patience: it is my ongoing dialogue with You. You have revealed this aspect of freedom in my life: nothing is useless because everything is a dialogue with You.' "

Or I can stand among those who do not understand; for now, it is the position that the Spirit is urging me to take. "Lord, please explain." Every time that I meditate on this parable, I say to myself: good, now I understand. But when I go back to my daily life, I just don't see, I don't have a sense of what it means, I don't understand. My spontaneous way of relating to others isn't like that. I understand the right way when I am doing my spiritual exercises, but outside of that, all my relationships with my neighbor are conflicted; I tend to be on the defensive and my goal is to keep my distance and my privileges.

We are all the same every time we foolishly refuse to see what the situation requires. Unfortunately, we are blind to reality. Sometimes we are blind even to the needs of those who are the closest to us. We are like the priest in the parable: he walks by the wounded man, but he is so used to it that he doesn't even see him.

And so, let us open up to the possibility of being won over in our blindness, willingly, authentically: "O Lord, when I was poor, tired, sick, imprisoned, did I ever sense your presence near me and feel moved by it? Much more often instead, I acted as if the situation entailed an excessive risk, or the need to defend myself, to keep a safe distance or to assert my rights." And this is what life is all about because it hinges on our relationship with others.

It is either a relationship that acknowledges the Lord, or one of giving and receiving—more or less for my own advancement; even if I don't step on others to get ahead, I still put myself first. Our entire existence rises to the surface here, if we are sincere and examine ourselves deep down in God's presence, even acknowledging our inability to change: "O Lord, one more meditation on this point will probably not open my eyes. Instinctively, in a combative situation, I pull back."

Life is full of conflicts in which we take a stand, keeping our distance and arming ourselves skillfully. From this point of view, we can honestly say: "It is true, O Lord, I am unable to recognize You. You give me the opportunity to do something charitable and generous, but my existence is far from being free, joyful, certain and loyal to You in all You ask, no matter how inordinate it may seem."

If we sincerely analyze our daily life and let it come to the surface for what it really is, the Lord will inspire us to be humble. Then, even after the fact, we can say: "Lord, I'm really sorry, but I didn't see You, I didn't hear You."

Why didn't I hear You? Was it only in a particular moment, was it a small misunderstanding? In that case, I can say: now I'm here, thank You, I understand. Or is my heart closed? Is there something in me that makes me opaque, inflexible, incapable of recognizing You? It is because our hearts have not been transformed by the Gospel, because we are always seeking what is right for us and a way to get ahead, and our neighbor is just a pretext for our good works.

Our inner blindness shows itself again. "Lord, I have eyes and do not see, I have ears and do not hear; I walk among the people as if You were not there." Or I might say: "Behold, You are here, here, and here, and that's enough; I have done too much already."

"I don't see You where You really are, but where it is convenient for me to see You; where habit, custom, tradition teach me to see You; otherwise, I am not sensitive enough to your presence and can't see You." We are in the dark and aware of it; only the Lord can free us.

We can ask Him in our personal prayer: "O Lord, teach me to understand: why am I not sensitive, why don't I know You? Or, why do I recognize You, quite willingly, in some circumstances, but not in so many others? So many times, I don't know, but my neighbors and friends know very well."

It happens so often, indeed: each one of us determines a particular sphere in which to practice honesty and justice, to the exclusion of all others; those around us can see that we are not aware of this or that, that we don't understand a certain situation and we don't pay attention to some other. And we ourselves are not aware of it.

And so we ask: "O Lord, I would like to see You, not only where I decide to see You, but also where others are calling my attention: why doesn't he see this, why doesn't he understand that, why doesn't he open his eyes?" This happens frequently even to saintly persons. Many people don't understand essential things: there are certain forms of complete insensitivity that can coexist with mystical fervor and great piety for decades, even an entire life; they harden the heart, blur the vision, and close the mind. Certain topics cannot be discussed: it's the inability to recognize the Lord's presence.

In such a situation and from inside the parable, this question is bound to arise: "Lord, what can I do? Do You want me to make more of an effort? Or do You want me to listen to your Word more attentively?" And with Matthew's Gospel in hand, let us seek the answer in the Gospel itself: "Lord, what is deep down inside ourselves? What burdens, closed-mindedness, and lack of transparency? What types of behavior prevent me from seeing You?"

Starting with this fundamental parable, we therefore ask the Lord for self-awareness. The meaning of our entire life and of the world itself is at stake: it's not enough to add a little aroma to our old wine, but we must make sure that the wineskin is in good condition, or else get a new one or an altogether different wine.

The Lord proposes a global vision of life that disrupts our convenient habits. Let us all pray to Him:

"Lord, let us be true to ourselves before the Church and the world. In that awareness of our true selves, make us accept what is hard, and closed, blind and opaque, all that makes us incapable of recognizing You within ourselves, all around us, in the world and its true requirements.

"Lord, remind us of all the times that we have rejected dialogue, closed our hearts, excluded possibilities.

"Lord, make us acknowledge You and all that You ask as king, shepherd, Christ, Son of Man, key to our life. Make us recognize your presence in our relationships, in history, in the Church and the whole world.

"Lord, we ask for ourselves only truth and authenticity; we ask that You vanquish in us the tyrannical and ever reborn enemies of this truth and authenticity. Help us not to fear the decisions that such authenticity implies and, without worrying about what we are, to live before You in the peace that truth brings.

"Your Spirit, O Lord, is a Spirit of peace: may we, in your peace, acknowledge what we are and what we are not; what You, in your love, are calling us to be, so that we may have the joy of becoming what You wish us to be.

"We thank You, Lord, for not letting us stagnate in the commonplace and in our own mediocrity; for inviting us to savor the joy of that 'little extra' that opens up new horizons.

"We thank you, Lord Jesus, for giving us your Spirit, You who ever shall live in a world without end. Amen."

A Grandiose View of the End of History

3 Blessed be God the Father of our Lord
Jesus Christ, who in his great mercy has
given us a new birth into a living hope
through the resurrection of Jesus Christ from
the dead 4 and into a heritage that can never
be spoiled or soiled and never fade away. It is
reserved in heaven for you 5 who are being
kept safe by God's power through faith until

> the salvation which has been prepared is re-
> vealed at the final point of time. 6 This is a
> great joy to you, even though for a short time
> yet you must bear all sorts of trials; 7 so that
> the worth of your faith, more valuable than
> gold, which is perishable even if it has been
> tested by fire, may be proved—to your praise
> and honor when Jesus Christ is revealed.
> 8 You have not seen him, yet you love him;
> and still without seeing him you believe in
> him and so are already filled with a joy so
> glorious that it cannot be described; 9 and you
> are sure of the goal of your faith, that is, the
> salvation of your souls. 10 This salvation was
> the subject of the search and investigation of
> the prophets who spoke of the grace you
> were to receive; 11 searching out the time and
> circumstances for which the Spirit of Christ,
> bearing witness in them, was revealing the
> sufferings of Christ and the glories to follow
> them. 12 It was revealed to them that it was
> for your sake and not their own that they
> were acting as servants delivering the mes-
> sage which has now been announced to you
> by those who preached to you the gospel
> through the Holy Spirit sent from heaven.
> Even the angels long to catch a glimpse of
> these things. —1 Pet 1:3-12

This passage, drawn from Peter's First Epistle, is full of theological perspectives, enthusiasm, and hope. As we read it, let us first try to grasp the structure of the text, which consists of three parts: the eschatological consciousness of Christians (vv. 3-5), the joy in the proof (vv. 6-9), the Messianic consciousness of Christians (vv. 10-12). They are, so to speak, three fundamental principles.

"Blessed be God, the Father of our Lord Jesus Christ" is what in Hebrew is called *berakah*, a blessing, which we know from other letters in the New Testament (for example, 2 Cor 1:3: "Blessed be God, the Father of our Lord Jesus Christ").

The blessing is followed by affirmative clauses that underline the principle and foundation of the Letter's exhortation: God "in his great mercy has given us a new birth into a living hope through the resurrection of Jesus Christ from the dead and into a heritage that can never be spoiled or soiled and never fade away" (1 Pet 1:3-4).

Peter's Hope-filled Message

The key word is hope, which is then specified in three ways: it is a heritage that "can never be spoiled or soiled and never fade away." Hope is absolutely untouchable and is definitive in nature. It's the experience of a vision opening onto eternity, not limited to the short-term goals of life on earth. We bless God for giving us this perspective that goes beyond death and reaches God's own completeness and happiness.

It's a living hope that "is reserved in heaven for you." After having said that God "has given *us* a new birth," Peter immediately switches to *you*: "It is reserved in heaven for *you* who are being kept safe by God's power through faith until the salvation which has been prepared is revealed at the final point of time" (vv. 4-5).

We marvel at the way in which the early Christian community was able to express the dogma so profoundly. Today, we wouldn't be able to write a sentence so dense with meaning. The ultimate goal is thus the living hope, which is eternal and is reserved in heaven by God's power, only to be revealed at the end of time. It is an eschatological hope, the principle and foundation of Christians, made certain by God and given to us through Jesus' resurrection from the dead.

A second fundamental principle derives from it: the joy in the midst of affliction (vv. 6-7): "This is a great joy to you, even though for a short time yet you must bear all sorts of trials, so that the worth of your faith, more valuable than gold, which is perishable even if it has been tested by fire, may be proved—to your praise and honor when Jesus Christ is revealed." Christians who are waiting for Jesus Christ's eschatological revelation can experience joy even in the trials of the present.

Right after the mention of Jesus Christ at the end of verse 7, we read a beautiful outpouring of love in verses 8 and 9: "You have not seen him, yet you love him; and still without seeing him you believe in him and so are already filled with a joy so glorious that it cannot be described; and you are sure of the goal of your faith, that is, the salvation of your souls."

This goes deeper into the fundamental truth: since everything hinges on the hope of what will come, and since hope fills the present with joy, loving Jesus also fills you with joy, even though you have not seen Him. This bliss springs from hope, love, and faith, and will be revealed at the end of time in the salvation of souls.

We notice that what is proclaimed as living hope in verse 3 is taken up again as faith in verses 7 and 9: "the worth of your faith, more valuable than gold;" "and you are sure of the goal of your faith." We also note that both parts end with a mention of eschatological salvation. Verse 5 says: "You are being kept safe by God's power through faith until the salvation which has been prepared is revealed at the final point of time;" and verse 9: "you are sure of the goal of your faith, that is, the salvation of your souls." These verses are thus a mystical contemplation of the eschatological salvation of Christians, and they express an awareness of the joy that it brings already now, in the present.

Verses 10-12 offer a third fundamental principle: understanding that we are the ultimate object of the salvific plan announced by the prophets of the Old Testament. Everything that has happened is about us: "This salvation was the subject of the search and investigation of the prophets who spoke of the grace you were to receive" (v. 10).

Verse 11 is considered a hermeneutical lens for reading the entire Bible: "they were searching out the time and circumstances for which the Spirit of Christ, bearing witness in them, was revealing the sufferings of Christ and the glories to follow them." Jesus' words to the disciples at Emmaus come to mind: the prophets had seen the suffering and glory of Christ and they have come true today for your sake (Lk 24:25-27).

This is said even more clearly in verse 12: "It was revealed to them that it was for your sake and not their own that they were acting as servants delivering the message which has now been announced to you by those who preached to you the gospel through the Holy Spirit sent from heaven. Even the angels long to catch a glimpse of these things."

We see in this verse a profound prophetic intuition of the meaning of the entire Old Testament, which is now fulfilled in Christians.

In conclusion, we can say that, to the principle and foundation constituted by the baptismal consciousness (1 Pet 1:1-2), Peter's First Epistle adds the principle and foundation constituted by the eschatological consciousness, the joyous awareness, we might say, of suffering as we contemplate eternal completeness, and of the messianic consciousness of being the final point in the history of salvation.

Before going on to the meditation, I would like to underline two key words in the text.

The first one, as I already mentioned, is the word "hope" (v.3): "a living hope," which repeats in 1:13:

"Hope to the end in that grace that is to be brought to you"; and will conclude the exhortation from chapter 1: "that your faith and hope might be in God" (v. 21).

Hope is the recurring theme of chapter 1.

Our Liberation

Another key word is "salvation": "You are being kept safe by God's power through faith until the salvation" (v. 5). The word is found again in verse 9: "You are sure of the goal of your faith, that is, the salvation of your souls," and in verse 10: "This salvation was the subject of the search and investigation of the prophets."

And so, it is not without reason that Saint Ignatius also uses "salvation" as a key word in his *Principle and Foundation*: "Man is created to praise, revere, and serve God our Lord and, by doing so, to save his own soul" (n. 23).

We find the same expression in number 177, where choice is discussed, which is at the very heart of the *Exercises* and can be made in all tranquility, "keeping in mind that man is born to praise God our Lord and to save his own soul"; and again in number 179 which says that I must choose "what seems to me better for the glory of God our Lord and the salvation of my soul."

We are no longer used to talking about the salvation of the soul, but we understand that it is a traditional term in the Holy Scriptures and in the Exercises, and that it signifies man's liberation from the danger of eternal death as his ultimate end.

Having read the text, I now suggest some reflections for your meditation.

If we ask ourselves to what extent eschatological hope is alive and present in the Church today, we must admit that it is somewhat forgotten. Sociological surveys give the impression that more than 50% of those who refer to themselves as Christians do not believe in eternal life or consider it as a possible appendix to human life. Their attitude can be summed up as follows: we must live well in this life and so much the better if there is another one! It is far from being a prospect on the eternal horizon which illuminates the present. The present is indeed illuminated by good values, but it is not seen in the vast perspective of eternity.

Maybe we were influenced by the mood created in the last century by Marxism that placed all hope for justice on this earth.

In my opinion, the disappearance of an eschatological horizon is a serious shortcoming of the Church in the West. All you have to do is compare the inscriptions found in cemeteries of the past, which always referred to the afterlife, with today's tombstones: at the very best, they mention that someone "lived a good life, was honest, loyal, a good Christian." No reference to eschatological hope.

Peter's Letter is a great reminder of what is missing in our Church. And we must remember that the hope of eternal life is not just hope for my own salvation, hope of "going to heaven," but hope that the Kingdom will be revealed, that the final judgment on history will show the glorification of the Risen Christ, that the moment will come when the whole of humanity acknowledges the kingship of Christ.

This hope inspires all our actions because it begins to be fulfilled as of now. The signs of its promise guide our pastoral and apostolic work. A bishop in particular is called upon to safeguard the great hope of the coming of the Kingdom and to direct the Church's action within the framework of this global vision.

I like to quote from Saint Paul's second letter to Timothy verses 4-8. I am struck by the expression "who have waited with love for his revelation," that is, not only are they waiting for it as the ultimate goal, but love it, wish for it, foresee it, and put it to work as of now.

The central verses 6-8 suggest the second theme for our meditation. If we keep in mind God's plan, the coming we are waiting for, it is easier to see the difficulties and hardships as purifying trials in preparation for the Kingdom. Such trials are not just normal setbacks or hard times that sooner or later are bound to happen, but rather means to prepare the total glorification of the name of Jesus in the world.

It's not by chance that Peter writes: through this suffering you "reach the goal of your faith: the salvation of souls" (v. 9). You will achieve the goal of your faith as of now if you live with a grandiose view of the end of history.

Appendix

The School of the Word

IT can hardly be denied, I think, that the western world is today experiencing a severe crisis of spiritual desolation. It no longer perceives the mystery of God as present in its major institutions and in the symbols that permeate its public life.

This interior aridity threatens everyone; in particular, it stifles Christians, who are unable to give expression in their daily lives to their faith in the living God. Beyond question, therefore, the Church must help the baptized to make the transition from a traditional faith based on habit and derived from the environment to a personal, interior faith based on conviction and capable of resisting the onslaught of secularism and atheism.

This kind of faith, understood as a dynamic process, is fed and deepened by hearing the word of God. From the very beginning of my episcopal ministry in Milan, my travels through the diocese made clear to me the need people have of the revealed word, their desire to join others in praying and listening to God's word, and the real feasibility of this kind of joint effort.

I also found a certain ignorance of Scripture among even the most highly educated. I therefore resolved to respond as best I could to the exhortation issued by Vatican II in its Constitution on Divine Revelation: that all of the faithful should have direct access to the Bible, because *contact* with the word of God brings an unsuspected wealth of life that is offered as a gift to every Christian. I myself have been reading the Scriptures for over forty years, and at every reading I am astonished to find them utterly new; at every reading I experience the jolt to mind and feelings that stirs a sense of human values and puts me in touch with the values of God.

I was convinced, then, that today, more than in times past, the pages of the Bible can deepen faith by awakening a consciousness of mystery, an openness to the infinite, a movement toward God, and an understanding of God's ways in history. I therefore developed a method that would enable the entire people of God to approach the texts of the Bible step by step.

This method I called the "School of the Word" or "School of Bible-Reading for the Masses." I began to use it with young people whom I invited to the cathedral on the first Thursday of each month. For five years in a row the young came by the thousands, and in ever increasing numbers, even from a distance and even from other dioceses. Their presence proved that the time we spent together (about two hours) in silence, listening to the word, and reflecting on the texts fed them interiorly.

This past year I suggested that these young people give what they have learned to other young people by setting up other "Schools of the Word" in various parts of the diocese. I then invited adults to the cathedral, and in particular laymen and laywomen who are involved in the life of the parish. Once again, the response was surprisingly good. I have also attempted during days of spiritual retreat, to teach children to select some passages from the Old and New Testaments and to understand them.

The "School of the Word" has gradually become a privileged tool of my pastoral activity and of my desire to foster, in communal form as it were, a holiness that is truly popular and not limited to an elite—a holiness that ignores class barriers, is developed in the most unexpected settings, and has the power to overcome all worldliness and fear.

What is a "School of the Word"? It is a step-by-step approach to the biblical text according to the ancient method of the Fathers, which in turn recalls the method of the rabbis and is known as *lectio divina* ("the reading of God's word").

In the Hebrew world the Scriptures were taught in the schools in a very simple way that was adapted to the people. At the same time, certain basic pedagogical and philological principles were operative, as well as a careful progression; if these principles and this progression were neglected, the teaching became fruitless and even counterproductive.

Here, briefly, are the *principles* and *method* of the pedagogy at work in *lectio divina*:

a) The *principles* governing the approach of the Christian people to the sacred text are four in number:

FIRST, *the unity of the Scriptures*. In a "School of the Word" the students must be made to realize that while the Bible is made up of many books it nonetheless forms a unity, inasmuch as every page speaks of God's great plan for the salvation of the human race. Everything refers to the paschal mystery. It is the effort to relate the various texts of the Bible to the unifying mystery that makes all of them yield a meaning, even those that at first glance have little to do with this mystery.

SECOND, *the humanness* or *"existential relevance" of the Scriptures*. The Scriptures speak to human beings; they give expression to the deepest treasures of the human heart, to the restlessness, sufferings, aspirations, desires, and fears that all human beings share. Individuals find themselves in the Bible, for it puts into words what is permanently human; it lends a voice to the human beings of every age as they speak of their hopes and their distresses. Through simple examples the people learn that the reading of Scripture helps them to that understanding of themselves as individuals and as a community, without which they cannot grasp their own unity or their true relationship to others.

THIRD, *the dynamic character of values*. The Bible expresses values that even today are still developing toward the future of humanity. From the viewpoint of the dynamic movement both of morality and of doctrine the Bible contains values that spur us to advance beyond ourselves by giving us a sense that we human beings are people on a journey. The Bible interacts with human life in a constant movement from life to the word of God and from the word of God back to life.

FOURTH, *the Scriptures are a real presence of Jesus.* A "School of the Word" must help people realize that when they read the Scriptures they can enter into a real communion with Jesus. The expression "real communion" may startle because it echoes the language applied to the eucharistic presence, but Vatican II does not hesitate to assert that the risen Christ is present in the Scriptures and that when we read them or listen to them we can experience this presence.

b) The *method* which Christian tradition has developed for *lectio divina* has four steps: reading, meditation, prayer, contemplation. The sequence is the result of theological and anthropological reflection on the way in which believers approach the word of God in order to assimilate it and make it bear fruit in experience and action.

FIRST, *reading*. The people learn to read and reread a passage by underlining and giving prominence to its key elements: the actions, verbs, acting subjects, attitudes and thoughts, settings, motives for acting. A careful study of all these produces a new and surprising understanding of the text because of the many points that are thus brought to light.

SECOND, *meditation*. In this second phase the people reflect on the abiding value of the passage, by trying to pinpoint the central value in it and its specific message in relation to history and context and situation. The students, whose aim is to discover their authentic selves and find God, single out the attitudes that emerge from the passage on which they are meditating: joy, fear, hope, desire, expectation, and so on.

THIRD, *prayer*. The students are gradually drawn to share the deeper religious sentiments that the text produces or suggests in the name of God; the values assimilated in meditation become motives for praise, thanksgiving, intercession, petition, forgiveness, and so on.

FOURTH, *contemplation*. At some point the multiplicity of sentiments, reflections, and prayers are reduced to unity in contemplation of the mystery of Jesus, the Son of God, a mystery that is contained in every page. This is especially true of the Gospels but it is also true in varying degrees of every passage in the Bible.

The aim, then, of the "School of the Word" is to try to read the word of God in such a way that it turns into prayer in us and sheds light on our lives. It is not possible, of course, to reach this goal in a single leap.

In order to stimulate the people to a prayerful listening to God's word, I usually read and reread a passage aloud, then suggest points for meditation, and, after this, remain silent for awhile. I then continue by praying on the passage I have read, thereby leading into a very simple form of personal contemplation.

It is most important for the people to see that the reading of God's word should make Christians challenge themselves: In what way are my life, my activity, my apostolate becoming a word of God in the light of the definitive Word that is Jesus Christ, present in the Scriptures? When they do this, the "School of the Word," which aims at bringing faith to bear on daily life, will express its radical power in certain interconnected attitudes. These are:

a) *Discernment*, that is, the ability Christians develop, with the grace of the Holy Spirit, to see in their lives what is or is not in conformity with the Gospel. It is a discernment of what is best, at a given moment in history, for themselves, for others, for the Church.

b) *Decision*, or the choice of what is in conformity with the Gospel in their lives.

c) *Action* which follows upon discernment and decision. Only the kind of Christian acting, doing, and thinking that is guided by the Holy Spirit can truly be called spiritual activity "according to God."

With the help of the "School of the Word," Christians will gradually become capable of recognizing, despite the ambiguities of history, the signs and glorious presence of the risen Lord in the midst of His people and the local community. My own experience with the "School of the Word" convinces me that it is a tool to be used by ordinary people, by any of the faithful who desire to live authentically Christian lives in a secularized world.

Life in this secularized world demands people who are contemplative, alert, critical, and courageous; it demands that from time to time they make new choices of a kind not made before; it demands attentiveness and new emphases to which they can be alerted by listening to God's word and being sensitive to the mysterious action of the Holy Spirit in hearts and in history.

Cardinal Martini, as archbishop of Milan, gave conferences to the American bishops gathered at Collegeville, Minnesota in June 1986. The translation of his article was prepared by Matthew J. O'Connell and reproduced in the May 1987 issue (Vol. 61, 5) of *Worship* and is reproduced here with the permission of the publishers.

NEW . . . DURA-LUX GIFT EDITIONS OF

THE NEW AMERICAN BIBLE

Supple material, blind embossing, foil stamping, precise stitching, and decorative gilding combine to provide an exquisite and unique package for the Word of God. The distinctive features of our St. Joseph Editions, incuding new maps, ribbon marker, and Family Record section, complete this unparalleled gift. Available in 7 luxurious colors. 1680 pages. Size 5½ x 8.

No. 609/19B Black Embossed Imitation Leather

No. 609/19BG Burgundy Embossed Imitation Leather

No. 609/19BLU Blue Embossed Imitation Leather

No. 609/19BN Brown Embossed Imitation Leather

No. 609/19GN Green Embossed Imitation Leather

No. 609/19W White Embossed Imitation Leather

No. 609/19C Red Embossed Imitation Leather

No. 609/51W White Embossed Bride's Bible

www.catholicbookpublishing.com

INSPIRATIONAL READING

ILLUSTRATED LIVES OF THE SAINTS

This collection includes a short biography of a Saint or Blessed together with a prayer for each day of the year, in accord with the *Roman Martyrology* (2004 edition). Four-color illustrations and a ribbon marker enhance this volume. 576 pages. Size $4^{1}/_{4} \times 6^{3}/_{8}$. **No. 860/22**

ILLUSTRATED LIVES OF THE SAINTS II

Companion volume to the *Illustrated Lives of the Saints.* 60 full-color illustrations and a ribbon marker enhance this attractively bound volume. 588 pages. Size $4^{1}/_{4} \times 6^{3}/_{8}$. **No. 865/22**

THE IMITATION OF CHRIST

Thomas à Kempis

This easy-to-read revised edition by Clare Fitzpatrick is the one religious book that is second only to the Bible in popularity. Large type. 40 full-color illustrations . 320 pages. Size $6^{3}/_{8} \times 9^{1}/_{4}$. **No. 322/22**

THE IMITATION OF CHRIST

Prayerbook Size Edition

This treasured book has brought peace to readers for many ages by showing how to follow the life of Christ to which all are called. 288 pages. Size $4 \times 6^{1}/_{4}$. **No. 320/23BG**

INTRODUCTION TO A DEVOUT LIFE

by Saint Francis de Sales

Adapted by Sr. Halcon J. Fisk

St. Francis, known as the apostle of love, reached out to everyone through this small book, showing that devotion is available to everyone. 128 pages. Size $4^{3}/_{8} \times 6^{3}/_{4}$. **No. 163/19G**

CONFESSIONS OF ST. AUGUSTINE

Translated by Rev. J.M. Lelen, Ph.D.

A Christian classic that—after the Bible and *The Imitation of Christ*—is the most widely translated and most universally esteemed. It is published in prayerbook format. 448 pages. Size $5^{1}/_{2} \times 8$.

No. 173/19BG or 173/19BN

www.catholicbookpublishing.com

SPIRITUAL LIFE SERIES

INSPIRATIONAL THOUGHTS FOR EVERY DAY

Rev. Thomas J. Donaghy

This book offers minute meditations for every day, which contains a Scripture quotation, reflection and prayer. 192 pages. Size 4 x 6¼. **No. 194/19**

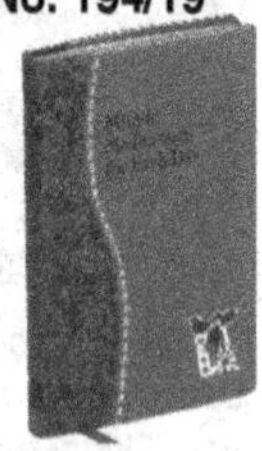

MINUTE MEDITATIONS FOR EACH DAY

Rev. Bede Naegele, O.C.D.

This book offers short Scripture text, a practical reflection and a meaningful prayer for each day of the year. 192 pages. Size 4 x 6¼. **No. 190/19**

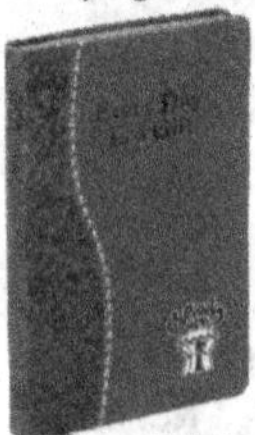

EVERY DAY IS A GIFT

Introduction by Rev. Frederick Schroeder

Popular meditations for every day, featuring a text from Sacred Scripture, a quotation from the writings of a Saint, and a meaningful prayer. 192 pages. Size 4 x 6¼. **No. 195/19**

DAILY MEDITATIONS ON GOD'S LOVE

Marci Alborghetti

Scripture verses, brief meditations, and prayers all focused on God's love for us. 192 pages. Size 4 x 6¼. **No. 183/19**

WORDS OF COMFORT FOR EVERY DAY

Rev. Joseph T. Sullivan

Short meditation for every day, including a Scripture text and a meditative prayer to God the Father. 192 pages. Size 4 x 6¼. **No. 186/19**

UPLIFTING THOUGHTS FOR EVERY DAY

Rev. John Catoir

We can eliminate negative thinking and improve our emotional life by filling our mind with uplifting thoughts. 192 pages. Size 4 x 6¼. **No. 197/19**

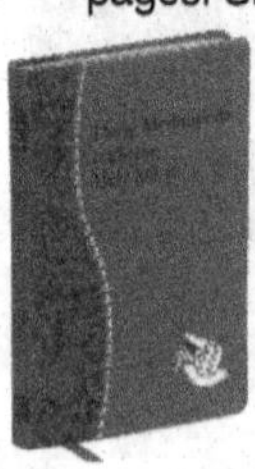

DAILY MEDITATIONS WITH THE HOLY SPIRIT

Rev. Jude Winkler, OFM Conv.

This book offers an opportunity to develop a closer relationship with the Holy Spirit and to apply this to our daily lives. 192 pages. Size 4 x 6¼. **No. 198/19**

www.catholicbookpublishing.com